W9-CYA-431

If I
Die
At
Thirty

If I Die At Thirty

Meg Woodson

ZONDERVAN PUBLISHING HOUSE
OF THE ZONDERVAN CORPORATION
GRAND RAPIDS, MICHIGAN 49506

IF I DIE AT THIRTY

Library of Congress Catalog Card Number 75-6182

Printed in the United States of America

To Peggie

I am not sure I can dedicate this book to Peggie Woodson, since in every way that counts it is already hers. But Joe, my husband, who has lived these conversations with me, and Joey, my son, who plays his own small but robust part, agree that I must try. For Peggie's strength is the book's strength, and in her sweetness lies any magic the book may weave. All the best lines are hers.

You've given this book to me, Peg. And now as best I can, I give it back to you — with all my love.

Contents

This is the most moving and effective book I have ever read about human affliction, especially involving a child. It soars far above anything I have ever encountered, partly because it is written with such consummate skill. Not a superfluous word, not a cliché, not a second of sentimentality. It made me smile and want to go on reading, even as it broke my heart.

As the mother of daughters myself, I know mother-daughter relationships at best can be very stormy. But to know that dear delightful nutty girl you laugh and fight and philosophize with is doomed — that she'll never make it to womanhood and you both know it — what could you teach each other about life and death? How could you comfort each other.

Well, the answers these two came up with have given me some invaluable answers in some of the most touching and revealing dialogues I have ever come across. They give a thoroughly inspiring picture of a Christian family courageously facing heartbreak.

IF I DIE AT THIRTY is a marvelous book — truly inspired. It is a book for every loving heart and deserves the widest possible audience.

— MARJORIE HOLMES

Preface

Cystic fibrosis is a hereditary disease affecting the mucus-secreting and sweat glands of the body. Normally mucus performs a valuable protective and lubricating function. In the C.F. patient it becomes thick and sticky, clogging and prohibiting the normal functions of the pancreas, intestines, salivary glands, and lungs; it produces malnutrition, diarrhea, abnormal sweating, and eventually fatal lung disease. National statistics show that 50 percent of children with this disease die before their fifteenth birthdays.

Peggie, our daughter, was born with cystic fibrosis. This book is based on conversations Peggie and her father and I had together between her thirteenth and fourteenth birthdays, conversations that began the day she discovered her limited life expectancy.

We share with you this slice of our life not to show Peggie's spiritual maturity or her parents' infallibility, but to demonstrate how even the most unfinished faith can work to ease — not to eliminate — the most poignant of human pains.

It's our suggestion that the book be read a chapter a day rather than at a single sitting, and it's our prayer that the reader will grow in his love for God in the reading as we have grown in our love for Him in the living. For in Peggie's words: "Some people might think it's a book about sorrow, but I prefer to think it's a happy book — a book about hope!"

Conversation About Early Death

"Everything Will Be Started But Nothing Finished"

Conversation About Early Death

Peggie danced her way into our bedroom, shortish blond hair flipping and large blue eyes sparkling with merriment. "Today I am five feet tall," she boasted, stretching to full height before her father. "For two years I've been four-feet-eleven-and-something, but this afternoon the doctor finally said it. *I am five feet tall.*"

She chattered gayly on about the doctor's latest card trick and giggled as she imitated how we'd tiptoed around the ladies' lounge so as not to waken the cleaning woman snoring there, bucket and mop by her side.

But she didn't mention the book she'd picked up in the waiting room — a coloring book designed to explain cystic fibrosis to children, but with a fine-print explanation at the end intended for parents. An explanation that Peggie, being Peggie, had read.

"Listen to this dumb book," she said, her tone hushed in deference to the crowded room. *"Children with C.F. do not have a normal life expectancy.* Don't they know that's only if you don't

15

have your therapy and all that? They could get sued for giving out false information, couldn't they, mother?"

My heart sank, and I couldn't reply immediately. All my years of preparation for this moment abandoned me on the spot. But my silence must have spoken truth to Peggie more sinisterly than any words could have, for as I glanced sideways at her face I saw a consternation on her tender, untried features that far outweighed my own.

"Kids like me are gonna live as long as anybody else. Right, mama?" she urged, her voice rendered almost inaudible by fear.

"Right, mama?"

I'd never lied to Peggie — not directly anyway. "Well, you probably won't live as long as grandmother and grandfather," I answered now in grossest of understatements. How glad I was that Joey, our eleven-year-old, was not with us, for he, too, had C.F. One child's moment of truth was all I could handle at a time.

Peg said nothing, but hung her head so her eyes couldn't meet mine, and two big tears splotched the coloring book in her lap.

"Didn't you know that, honey?" I asked, putting my hand gently on her arm.

"I never dreamed it." Peggie was not one for emotional scenes in crowded rooms, and she pulled away from me into the far corner of her chair.

I thought maybe she'd let it slide, but later in the hospital cafeteria she looked at me over her hamburger, eyes expressionless. "How long?" she asked.

"How long what?"

"If I'm not gonna live as long as grandmother and grandfather, how long?"

I made believe I was having trouble swallowing my cheese sandwich, and I was. But it was more the lump in my throat that wouldn't go down. "Well," I gulped, "lots of children with C.F. are living into adulthood and getting married and

16

having children of their own these days. Dr. Rathburn says a lot of you are going to be at his funeral."

Peg dropped the subject again, but I knew it was never out of her consciousness from the way it kept appearing in our conversation out of nowhere. Like when we were driving home in the car. "How about thirty?" she'd interjected, apropos of nothing. "Will I live to be thirty?"

So I knew it was on her mind as she stood by our bed that night and turned her bubbly fizz of words at me.

"You know, mother, I been wonderin' what I should be when I grow up. I mean I can't decide 'cause sometimes I want to be a writer but sometimes I want to be a teacher of handicapped children."

This couldn't go on.

"You're troubled, aren't you, Peg?" I asked, and she threw herself on the bed between Joe and me, sobbing.

"If I die at thirty, there won't be time to finish anything. Everything will be started but nothing finished." She may have been five feet tall, but she cried with the abandon of a small child.

I gathered her close, patting her shoulder helplessly, grateful for the soothing sound of Joe's voice. "If we do God's will every day we live," he was saying gently, "we don't have to worry about when we die because whenever it is, we can know we've finished everything God thinks it's important for us to do. Jesus had something to say along these lines, remember? *It is finished.* Those were His words, Peg, and He was only thirty-three."

"But if I die at thirty, you and mama will probably still be here and I won't get to see you guys." Peggie almost choked on the words.

"Maybe not," I took courage from Joe, "but New York grandmother and grandfather may well be in heaven waiting for you, and Memphis grandmother and grandfather too."

I tried to explain about time being relative in the next life, but she couldn't understand this. A fact which wasn't surprising, since I couldn't understand it myself. "At any rate," I finished, "time is different in heaven. The Bible says a thousand years with the Lord are as a single day. Why we'll all be together again almost before you know you've been away from us.

"And anyway, if there's one thing nobody ever misses in heaven, it's love." I knew I was babbling on and on, fearing silence more than anything else. Yet I couldn't help myself. "Can you imagine anyone being lonely or uncared for in heaven?" I asked. "Remember the story I told you once about the girl who was dying, and just before she died she talked to her father about the crowds of children that came running out of heaven to meet her?"

"Now I know why you were tellin' me all those stories," Peggie said. "I remember that one. All the kids ran up to her and hugged her and wanted to walk with her."

"Just think," I said, "no more mean kids calling you names or knocking your books down under the grandstands."

"But there are nice kids, too. You and daddy are always talking about how great heaven is, but I like it pretty much here."

"Well, I'm glad you do," I replied. And we like it pretty much having you here, too, I added to myself. Wasn't it all of us liking it pretty much having her here that made it so hard — so terribly, terribly hard? "But this life is kind of like a trip," I pressed. "You know what a good time we have every summer going to see New York grandmother? All those Howard Johnson's on the turnpike and the books and games in the car? We have a wonderful time, but all the while we know we're going someplace and the best time is waiting for us when we get there."

"Death can look pretty awful," Joe put in, only the strain in his voice indicating how hard all this was on him. "It's like when we get off the turnpike and all those bridges and parkways are twisting this way and that, and it's a new experience for us and we think we'll never get through. But we do because we know that finally when we get to *my father's house* he'll have the yard all fixed up for croquet and grandmother will have homemade chicken soup waiting. We know *a place will be prepared* just for us."

Peggie was staring at Joe, her eyes wide and misty. "But if I die at thirty and I'm married and have children, I won't get to see them grow up."

"We can't tell you it's going to be easy," Joe said softly.

For myself, I just lost control and put my face down next to Peg's and cried with her. I knew how she felt about not watching her children grow up.

Peggie had been six months old when the diagnosis of cystic fibrosis was made. And Joey after her. In those days the prognosis wasn't as hopeful as it is now. "Your children have a fifty-fifty chance of living to be five," our local doctor said. "And no chance of outliving childhood."

But I'd been thirty when Peggie was born. We'd waited too long for our children to accept such a verdict without a fight. C.F. did, after all, come in all degrees of severity. Maybe our local doctor was wrong; maybe Peg and Joey had a mild case.

We took them to the leading pediatrician at the best medical center in our area of the country. "Take them home and enjoy them," he said.

We tried. It wasn't easy, though. Every moment of our enjoyment of their babyhood, their toddler days, and their sturdy young childhood was marred by our fear that each stage of their development might be their last.

"Is there anything I can do to make it longer besides take all my pills?" Peggie's tremulous tones interrupted my thoughts.

"Well, you can try harder to cough stuff up and you can exercise more," I said, prodding almost automatically. It wasn't really a prodding, though. It was a hope and a prayer.

"The doctors might find a cure for C.F. any time now," Joe added, and his words were another hope and prayer. "And God is healing a lot of people directly these days, too. Why, we had a man in our last church who was operated on for cancer when he was fifty-five. But the cancer was so bad the doctor just closed him up and sent him home to die. And he did die — thirty years later of a heart attack."

"Now he's one who did go to his doctor's funeral," I added. "He used to laugh about it all the time."

"If God wants me to," Peggie declared, "I'll live longer than anybody in the whole world."

"Right!" Joe and I chorused, and it came out so loudly that we all grinned self-consciously at each other.

But Peggie's grin faded quickly. "I still wish I hadn't read that book. There'll never be a day I don't think about it. Nothing will ever be the same."

Then Joe told Peggie about Saint Francis who'd been hoeing his garden one day when somebody asked him what he'd be doing if he knew it was the last day of his life. Saint Francis had said, "I'd be hoeing my garden." He was hoeing his garden to the glory of God. What better thing could he do?

I pulled Peg's head down on my shoulder and wiped the moist hair back from her forehead, and she relaxed a little against me. She might not appreciate it now, I thought, but she could be one of the lucky ones. Most people don't think about death, so they don't live their lives in perspective. But isn't the time all of us live before we die terribly short compared to the time we are going to live after we die? Peg wouldn't be able to forget about death so easily. Well, good. We'd have long conversations on every aspect of the subject that she wanted to talk about. Nothing would be hushed up again.

"But if I die at thirty, I've lived half my life already."

"When you were a little girl," I told her, "I wrote a prayer for you. It went like this:

> I pray that Peggie will live long, dear God.
> But if not long, I pray she will live well,
> Three years perhaps or thirty-three,
> But years that will be somehow finished
> When she hears Thy bell.
> I pray that Peggie will live well for Thee."

"Oh yeah, that's right. I forgot daddy said that already."

"Did you know that the poets Shelley and Keats and Byron all died in their twenties and thirties?" Joe asked, seizing the opportunity. "Yet they rank among the outstanding writers of all time."

"And Joan of Arc was still a teen-ager when they burned her at the stake," I added quickly, "but today she's Saint Joan."

"You're makin' it sound like it's better to die young again," Peggie complained, her mouth drooping.

"Oh, honey," I said, hugging her tightly, "one thing you can be sure of is that we're doing every single thing we can to see that you live as long as possible. You're getting the best medical care available anywhere. And everybody we know is praying for you. You may live to be as old as Methuselah. We just want to be sure you understand that God has a plan for you and that your life can be worthwhile no matter how long you live."

I was tempted then to go on and tell her about Methuselah who had lived to be the oldest man in the Bible but about whom practically all the Bible said was that he lived 969 years and died. I wanted to stress that old age in itself wasn't all that important, but I found myself stirring restlessly, sensing we'd said enough for one occasion.

Peggie mistook my restlessness as a signal for bedtime. "I don't think they have night in heaven," she said. "I don't think you go to bed there. Now that would be neat." We all laughed a little then, shakily, but we laughed, our arms around each other in a kind of huddle.

We stayed that way for a while talking about familiar things — a new pair of jeans Peggie wanted, what we'd done on Easter vacations past and what we would do on the one soon coming up, and her hopes for highest honors at school. And as we talked, physically we pressed even closer to one other.

We'd said too much, hadn't we, I thought. Tried too hard to impart too much wisdom all at once? Dear Lord, how can we tell? Yet perhaps Peggie would remember something of what we'd said, retain something of the sense of spiritual security we'd been trying to impart, if we could reinforce it now with our own body warmth, with the kind of safety she could visualize of at least the immediate future — if we could envelop her now with the certain closeness of our own love.

We did our best.

And Peggie went off to her bed and to sleep. And Joe and I went to ours, and Joe lay next to me weeping quietly. Then he stopped and clambered out of bed. "I'm going to make sure she's all right," he said. Soon he was back, but only to repeat and repeat the whole performance.

It was a strange sound, the sound of Joe's weeping — a sound I hadn't heard in nineteen years of marriage. I found it frightening in its strangeness, but comforting in a way. For I knew why Joe was crying. He had grieved over Peggie before, but his grief had always been for himself, for the loss he was to know. Now he was hurting as only a father could for the hurt of his beloved daughter. It added something to my concept of fatherhood.

And I lay there, too limp to cry, thinking of the God who preferred above all names the name of Father, the God whose cherished daughter I was. Was He grieving with me, I wondered? Hovering especially near? Checking on me through the night?

"I'm all right," I told Him. "We're all all right."

Conversation About Healing

"If God Does Make Me Well"

Conversation About Healing

"Will you rock me, mama?"

Perhaps a peculiar request from a young teen-ager, but in our family we *touch* a lot, and I gladly walked with Peggie up the stairs to the rocker in her room.

"I don't really care if God heals my cystic fibrosis at this meeting or not," she had said the night before as we'd walked down the stairs. "I mean if God doesn't make me well, I'll just go to heaven sooner." Yet as I'd stopped and impulsively sheltered my daughter in my arms, as I'd felt the tightening of her whole slight body, it had seemed I was holding hope personified.

It had all been her idea. She had heard about the healing service; she had begged to go.

"Oh, can we, mother? Can we go? Please, mother?"

How could I say no? I believed in spiritual healing. I'd had too much experience with it myself not to believe in it. Didn't Peg deserve to make her own decision in this matter? Yet Joe and I had already gone the healing meeting route with our

children. And there was a big difference between believing in spiritual healing and approving of all the emphases and excesses of some healing meetings. Could I subject Peggie to the same destructive sense of guilt and rejection we'd experienced at those times? My reluctance persisted.

Yet in the end Peg's importunity could not be denied. She'd dressed carefully, choosing her green plaid pants, red turtleneck, and owl pendant for all the world like she was going on her first date. How excitedly she chattered in the car, ignoring my carefully chosen words of caution. And when finally we found a place to sit in the balcony of the large church, how confidently she perched on the edge of her seat, her flat chest rising and falling with quickened expectancy. I thought my heart would burst with my longing and my fear for her.

At the end of the sermon she had risen from her seat and walked to the communion rail as though she'd been waiting all her life for just that moment.

"And what would you like God to do for you?" the minister had asked.

"I have cystic fibrosis."

I knew even then it would be with me forever — the moment when the minister performed the age-old ceremony of the laying on of hands and prayed that God would take Peg's C.F. all away. And the next moment, too, when we sat back in our seats and I felt Peg trembling beside me.

"What's the matter, honey?" I'd whispered.

"I think I still have it," she'd whispered back.

Would my heart always melt like this at the memory of those words? Had I been right to expose the child to such trauma?

"You're not mad 'cause I got sick at school and came home today, are you?" she asked me now as we reached the top of the stairs.

"No, honey, I'm not mad," I said, stopping for a moment to give her a reassuring hug. And then I told her about once when her father and I had taken her to a healing service back when she'd been too little to know what was going on and I'd had to get up quickly right in the middle of the meeting and find a ladies' room to keep from *getting sick* all over the sanctuary.

"Aren't we two dummies, though?" I asked, "Getting sick at meetings where people are supposed to be getting well?" I could sense Peg's relief as we laughed together.

Peggie sleeps in a mist tent at night, and most days her bed is turned back with bedding hung this way and that to dry. But today had been wash day, and her bed was all put back together, the tiny blue flowers in her sheets and matching comforter blending with the blue of her room.

"I love my bed when it's like this," she exclaimed as we walked in. "So normal!"

"You know, Peg," I said as she settled in my lap, "I think you *do* care that God didn't make you well, and I think it's important that you admit this to yourself."

She thought this over for awhile as we rocked quietly. "You mean this is another of those subconscious things and that's why I'm sick to my stomach?" she asked.

I nodded my head, moving in rhythm with the rocking. "Remember last night when you said, 'I think I still have it?' Well, you were crying when you said it."

"I was in the school library today," Peggie responded, her voice flat, almost as though she were talking about someone else, "and I was workin' in a little alcove by myself and this boy, Eugene, came in and he was foolin' around with my books and he wouldn't stop buggin' me and finally he said, 'Peggie Woodson, are you dying yet?' He says that all the time, and I hate it."

"I was reading a column by Billy Graham the other day, and even he said that as much as we long to go to heaven and be with Jesus, we still have an instinctive, God-given desire to hang onto life."

"You mean 'cause I know it here and I don't know it there?" All at once I felt Peggie's body vibrate with her crying. "Okay," she said finally, "I guess I do care. I know I got up about four o'clock this morning to take some medicine and my stomach hurt so bad I had this crazy thought, *Maybe He's healing me now.* You know they said it might happen later, and I did get pretty excited when I thought that. I guess I do want to be like everybody else.

"You got that, subconscious?" she asked, tapping her forehead. "I do care.

"But I'm not afraid, mama. I'm honestly not. I used to be afraid all the time — of God and death and things — but ever since I found out I might not live long and daddy talked to me that night, I'm not scared any more."

How glad I was that my daughter had Joe for a father, and with deep satisfaction I remembered what a friend had told me just a couple days before. "Know what your Peggie said to my Becky last week when they were having the garage sale? Right out of the blue she said, 'If you ever get leukemia or anything like that, Becky, you come and tell my father and he'll talk to you out of the Bible so you won't be afraid to die. It's kind of like a course he gives.' " We had laughed together. Yet Peggie's childlike faith had inspired my own.

"And I'm not sorry I went to the meeting either," she declared now. "I mean last night when I was in bed I just laid there being happy all over. Not for myself, but for all the people who got what they wanted."

"It's good to be happy for other people, isn't it?"

"Well, I kept seeing Mrs. Williams' face. I never saw a face shine like that. She was so close to God she didn't care one way or the other about her arthritis. And that woman right in front of me? Oh, mother, when she sat in that chair and held out her legs, I saw one of them was shorter than the other. And then when the minister prayed for her, I saw her leg grow. I mean it's one thing to say you believe in miracles, but it's something else to stand right next to one. Her leg just went bloo-ooop."

As I'd laid in his arms the night before, I had talked to Joe about Mrs. Williams and about the woman whose leg apparently had been lengthened. We'd both wondered how Peg would react to the fact that God had not responded to some people while He'd responded so directly to others, either spiritually or physically. Her answer, as I put the question to her now, revealed that she, too, had given the matter serious consideration.

"Well," she said in her most grown-up tones, "for one thing, you know kids today are not like they were in the old days. There are some kids today who never would believe in God unless He did something spooky to them. You know how they're always wanting to be high and things.

"And I think, too," she added, "maybe the reason God didn't come to me that way was 'cause I already had Him more. I mean you can't very well have a minister like daddy for a father and not have the Holy Spirit seep into you all your life. And that night when I found out I might not live long and daddy talked to me, the Holy Spirit really came to me that night."

We were silent for awhile. I don't know what Peg was thinking, but I was thinking how strongly I disagreed with the persistent theory that it was the most saintly Christians for whom God performed the most supernatural acts. My own observation was that often it happened the other way around — that God used miracles more or less to hook people, to get them started in the Christian life. Then the closer they got to Him, the less inclined He seemed to be to take away the bad things that happened. Instead, He seemed more inclined to use those happenings to bring His people even closer.

"Did it bother you, Peg," I asked, "that the minister acted like everybody would be healed?"

"Well, it was when he was tellin' all the stories about the people who got healed in his other meetings that I really got my hopes up. I think to be fair he should have told stories about some people who didn't get healed, too."

"Maybe we should write him a letter and tell him how we feel."

"Oh, mother, could we? He was so nice. I think he'd like to know. Could I help write the letter? Some of the people looked so disillusioned. There was one woman in a wheelchair, and I could see she believed she would walk and she couldn't and she cried."

Peggie squirmed a bit and settled down more comfortably on my lap. "Actually, mother, I think finding out about my life span has been the most significant thing that's ever happened to me spiritually." Peg reads avidly and sometimes expresses herself maturely for her years. "I mean I might have learned the things I've learned anyway, but it sure would have taken a lot longer. I don't think we should tell Joey yet, though. I don't think I could have handled it in the fifth grade.

"You know, mother," she went on, and I noticed she had to work at keeping her voice from shaking, "I been thinkin'. I don't believe God hasn't healed me all this time because He doesn't love me, but because He does. I think He wanted me to learn all the things I've learned."

"Now that's a good point," I assured her. "You know this furniture mother and daddy just gave you?" I asked, suddenly inspired by the white and gold dresser and desk that had been the gift of a lifetime and given at great sacrifice. "Suppose the only time you felt we loved you was when we did something spectacular like that for you and not in the humdrum or hard times? You wouldn't be a very healthy child emotionally."

"You mean some people kind of wait from miracle to miracle and don't feel God loves them in-between? Mmmm — now I think that's a good point.

"But I still think the most important thing," she said conclusively, "is that if God doesn't make me well, I'll just be with Him sooner. And if God does make me well — "

"Oh, Peggie," I interrupted, "don't say that. *If* — *if* God makes you well. How many thirteen-year-olds do you think there are who are as *well* as you?" I hugged my daughter to me, this beautiful child who one brief month ago had been interested primarily in advancing the cause of Peggie Woodson.

"And if God does make me well," she persisted, "I'll just be here longer to do more good for people. I know I care, mother. I know I care. But it's still okay either way."

She pulled away from me and sat erect, looking down at her middle. "You got that, stomach?" she called loudly. "It's okay either way."

Oh, God, I breathed, *help me to be as strong as she.* And help my love to be as tough as Yours. Oh, God, if You make her well — or if You don't.

Conversation About Why

"Don't Worry About What Caused It — Just Worry About The Result"

Conversation About Why

"Oh, does that make me mad!" Peggie pounded the kitchen table so hard her milk sloshed over the rim of her glass and onto the red checkered tablecloth. We'd been sitting there, contentedly I thought, munching bedtime snacks — she Twinkies and I carrot sticks — and listening to a local radio program Joe emcees. This Sunday he had interviewed parents of mentally retarded children.

"Why did God make my child retarded? Why did God send that tornado? Why did God give me C.F.?" Peggie mimicked as she turned off the radio. "Why do people always say that? God didn't do any of those things."

Quick tears burned my eyes. How carefully I'd refrained from bringing up the question of why Peg had C.F. —*why* not in the physical, but in the metaphysical sense. Somehow I'd felt I couldn't bear it if she pointed the accusing finger at God. But here she'd brought up the subject herself, and the only finger she pointed was at the people who pointed the finger at God.

"Don't they know He's not like that?" she cried indignant-

35

ly. "He planned everything to be good. He wouldn't do mean things like that." She had on her bright blue pajamas, and her eyes blazed royally to match.

"And then," she went on, "they say God did this or that mean thing to make them better people. That's dumb. You know there's one thing I hate about C.F. camp. Half the kids there don't even believe in God. I don't know about Joey's side, but on the girls' side it's like they've said, *God gave me C.F. — Good-by, God.*"

"Yes, but you have to admit you've become a better person since you found out about your limited life expectancy," I told her. "Remember how we were talking after the healing service about how much you'd changed? Well, you haven't stopped yet."

"How have I changed?" she challenged. But I could tell she knew she had and just wanted her improvements listed.

"Well, it used to be that no matter how pleasant I was with you, you were unpleasant in your response. You practically never spoke to me without putting me down. But now even when I'm unreasonable with you, you're reasonable with me. Sometimes I just can't believe it."

"Har! Har! Har!" It was Joey's voice from where he sat at the dining room table working a jigsaw puzzle. "Peggie reasonable? Har! Har! Har!"

"Quiet, brat!" Peggie yelled, but playfully.

"If you want proof you've changed," I said, "just look at your relationship with Joey. Why, you two haven't thrown medicine bottles at each other in I don't know how long."

"I've had an accelerated course in adolescence," Peg said smugly, but with what seemed to me extraordinary discernment.

And then she began rolling her eyes and pointing to the next room, and we both fell silent as we realized Joey had probably heard our whole conversation.

"When you said I had a limited life expectancy, you meant of course if I didn't take all my pills," she bellowed.

"Oh, Peg," I whispered, "thanks a lot."

"Well, it's true," she whispered back. "I mean in a way it's true — sort of, it's true?" She grinned at me impishly, and I couldn't help chuckling in response, fine moral influence that I was.

"Bearing in mind your obvious lack of perfection," I said meaningfully, "what do you think God could have let happen to bring about more improvement in you more quickly?"

"There must have been a lot less drastic way to do the work."

"What?"

"Well, it wouldn't have had to be this bad or permanent."

"Oh, come on. If it weren't as serious, do you really think it would have done as much good?"

"You got me stumped," she admitted. "But you don't think God made it happen, do you?"

"Well, what do you think?" I asked her. "If you divided the general population into Christians and non-Christians and figured the percentage of each that had children with C.F., would you come out with even or uneven percentages?"

"I don't think God interferes with things like that unless He has a big drastic reason," she said nonchalantly and began attacking her box of Twinkies in earnest.

I, of course, sat there trying to figure the whole thing out philosophically, remembering how long before Peggie had been born, before even the egg and sperm that formed her had come together, I'd prayed that God would control the genes that went into the making of Margaret Ann Woodson. We hadn't known about cystic fibrosis then. And later when we did and thought about having a second child, and the doctor told us we had three out of four chances of having a healthy one, we really prayed God would control the odds. And then Joey had been born with C.F. too. Now I didn't think God had made it happen, but He surely hadn't stopped it either. He had let it happen.

I pointed these things out to Peg. Perhaps I should have left well enough alone. Perhaps it wasn't right to test her. I guess I just wanted to make sure her faith was as sound as it seemed to be, to reassure myself. I think too, though, I wanted to prepare her for the deeper questioning that sooner or later would come her way.

"Well," she responded, "God's not going to work you like puppets. We have to work ourselves. I mean you and daddy took the chance. You can't blame God for that. I think a lot of people blame God for things they could stop if they wanted to. Like they blame God for pollution, and they're sittin' there addin' to the mess."

"But why do you think He lets evil happen to people who aren't responsible for that particular evil?" I asked, pressing the test one step further.

"You sure are full of questions." Peggie looked at me curiously.

"Well, they aren't just my questions," I pointed out. "They're questions philosophers have asked all through the ages. *If God is all-powerful and if He loves us, why doesn't He stop the evil in the world?*"

"Well, my goodness, mother, if He was gonna stop one mother from havin' a sick kid, He might as well stop all mothers from havin' sick kids. He might as well stop all the bad things in the world. Then it would be the end of the world, and He's not ready for that.

"I mean," she continued, "if He made things perfect and the people were still bad, they'd think God wasn't really there and they were doin' things themselves, and the people would get worse and worse. And pretty soon the world would be bad again and God would have to keep fixin' it up and fixin' it up, and what would be the point of it?"

How effortlessly it poured forth, this native wisdom of Peg's. Not that I was about to admit to simple, final answers to the questions at hand. Yet it seemed to me Peg was doing as well as anyone else I'd come across lately. Better than most. How I longed to keep her exactly as she was, this half-child, half-woman daughter of mine. I only wished my mind were as uncluttered as hers.

It was a fantastic, magnificent world in which we lived, but a world in which something fundamental had obviously gone wrong. A wrongness — a sin — that affected the process of all of our lives. Why did we fight it so, we grown-ups, our inevitable involvement in the gone-wrongness of the world?

And what earthly reason did we have to place the blame on God? It took a twisted, adult mind to do that. For He'd made a perfect world, hadn't He? And when we spoiled that one, hadn't He prepared another perfect world for us? And hadn't He provided all the resources we needed to make it in-between the two unspoiled worlds?

"We asked Mr. Anderson once why didn't God take all the evil out of people," Peggie said, referring to our Sunday school superintendent. "What's the answer? I can't remember what he said. I guess with some people their whole character is built on evil and no personality would be left. I mean if we said, 'Stop everything evil, God,' God would be controlling us. Or," she added thoughtfully, "we'd be controlling Him.

"Anyway, we're not really lovin' Him if we're lovin' Him just 'cause He doesn't let anything bad happen to us or makes all good things happen. I think that's what it's all about. He doesn't want to control us. He wants us to love Him because we want to love Him.

"Some people say," she added, " 'I'll be Your person, God, if You do such and such for me.' Now that would be blackmail. God doesn't bargain."

Rarely had I seen Peggie hold forth so long on any one subject — or so seriously. Evidently my not mentioning it had not kept her from thinking about it.

"It's like what you said before, mother. If nothin' bad ever happened, it wouldn't be good for people. I mean if people were good, nothin' bad would have to happen to keep 'em good. But as long as people are bad, bad things have to happen to make 'em good."

I'd just been reading *Jesus Rediscovered* by Malcolm Muggeridge and remembered one of his comments on the presence of evil in the universe. "There is no catastrophe, as it seems to me, that can befall human beings which is not an illumination."

I tried that one out on Peg.

"Huh?" she said.

"Well, it's sort of the same thing we've been saying right along, the same thing the Bible says when it insists everything that happens to us can have a purpose, that God can work it together for our benefit."

"The Bible says it too? You're kiddin' me. Where?"

"Go get a Bible."

"Where's the closest one?" she cried and ran for my study, coming back with a *Good News for Modern Man.*

"Here it is," I said, leafing my way to Romans 8:28. " 'For we know that in all things God works for good with those who love him, those whom he has called according to his purpose.' "

"It says it!" Peggie shouted. Rarely had I seen her so excited.

"Does it say it works that way for all people?" I asked. "Careful now."

"Now I see. It can go either way, like the kids at C.F. camp." She grabbed a pencil, tore off a piece of napkin, and scribbled *Romans 8:28* down on it. "I'm gonna hang this on my bulletin board," she said.

Even I, accustomed as I was to Peggie's bursts of enthusiasm, was amazed at the strength of her reaction. I'd always tried to be soft sell with her as far as the Christian faith was concerned, as she normally reacted negatively to the kind of direct teaching I'd just been doing. And here she was acting for all the world like I'd handed her Christmas and her birthday rolled into one. Had she been longing that hard for some basic design for the brief span of her existence?

I just sat there looking at her as she rolled her Twinkie wrappings into balls and lined them up in size order. It seemed my heart could not contain the love it held for her or my own intense desire that the all-too-brief span of her existence be lived *according to plan.*

"It's living without meaning that drives people mad," I told her softly. "We can live with anything as long as it has a purpose, especially a purpose as big as the universe itself."

"What's exactly the purpose?"

"Well, why do you think we're here? Why were you born?"

"I think — I think I'm here to keep God company."

And then she added, "You know, I've noticed that preachers and even teachers keep saying we should ask ourselves *Who am I? Who am I? Go back to your homes and think about these things.* It's so dumb, and nobody knows what they're talkin' about. Is that what it's all about? I'm God's child, and I'm here to keep Him company?"

"Yes, though of course we're here to work for Him and our fellow human beings, too."

"Well, that's part of being God's child. But I can't believe it's so simple. Why does everybody talk like it's so complicated? An awful lot of people go through all that trouble and never find the answer."

"Well, now you know what your purpose is. And the point to which this discussion seems to be leading is that if we let Him, God can use C.F. or anything that happens to us to help us better fulfill that purpose, to make us better children of His, and to enable us to keep Him better company."

"We have to think about these things, mother. I mean when Charlie Yellow died, I knew the Bible said God cared about birds and knew when a sparrow fell, but when daddy read it out of the Bible — I felt it. Is that why daddy reads *Words of Comfort* all the time, so he'll feel them?"

"Why do you think — "

"Oh, mother, stop!" she cried. "Stop, stop, stop, stop! You're exhausting me with these questions. I never thought I'd say this, but please may I go to bed? I think we should just trust God. People are always saying, 'Why doesn't God do this? Why doesn't God do that?' Why don't they just try trusting Him? I mean He's God.

"Anyway," she went on, "I don't see the point to all these whys. Not since you showed me Romans 8:28. I mean if it all can work out better in the end, then don't worry about what caused it. Just worry about the result.

"Now I suggest, mother," she said as she sailed grandly out of the room, shorty pajamas notwithstanding, "that you try telling your philosophers that."

I just might, Peg, I thought proudly. I just might.

*Conversation About How
Much God Understands*

"It's Real Neat To Have A God Who Cares About Stuff Like That"

Conversation About How Much God Understands

"Mother, you absolutely must take me to Kresge's today." Peggie swirled through the front door and cascaded down the basement steps.

"And what precisely has Kresge's got that I haven't got?"

"Earrings that look like apple cores! Can you imagine, mother?"

"No, I can't imagine, daughter."

"Well, Janet had a pair on at school today, and they are so adorable. They look just like real apple cores and they're for pierced ears and Heidi got her ears pierced just before she moved away and if I don't mail them today she won't get them in two days which," she paused for effect, "happens to be her birthday."

"In that case let us proceed without delay," I said, shutting off the iron, clicking my heels, and heading up for the garage.

"Boy, are you in a good mood," Peggie cried, scurrying after me. "What happened?"

"Well, Heidi's your friend," I replied, ignoring the cheekiness of her question and the feigned innocence of her voice. "You know they always say *anything for a friend.*"

It was a careless remark, and yet as I sat in the car waiting for Peggie to buy her apple cores the words echoed in my mind, and I couldn't help remembering all the years when we literally would have given almost anything for a friend for Peggie.

We had kept Peg isolated as a toddler. "Keep her away from anybody with a fresh cold," the doctor said. "And any time you hear of red measles anywhere around, don't let her out of the house." That was all we had to hear. We kept Peg away from almost everybody almost all the time. So when she started school, she was set apart not only by her illness but by her inability to relate to other children as well.

"Peggie's a loner," Miss Andes, her first-grade teacher, told us.

"Peggie puts her studies first," said Mrs. Ottawa in the second grade. "Why when I look in at lunch, the other girls are laughing in a group, but Peggie sits there by herself with her nose in a book."

We had birthday parties for Peggie and the girls she asked came, but when they had parties they rarely asked Peggie back. "Jody's having a sleep-over next week," Peggie'd say. "I know 'cause Kim and Mary Ann got invitations today."

We encouraged her to join the Brownies, but "the kids were so mean" she only went when we made her.

"We took a trip to the museum today," a third-grade Peggie told us. "We chose partners for the bus. I sat with Mrs. Peterson."

Peggie became more and more arrogant in her attitude toward her schoolmates, pretending she didn't want to be friends with *them.* But we knew she cared. Oh, how she cared. And how we cared. Never did loneliness hold more vulnerable a captive, or a captive more heartsore an audience.

In the fifth grade she ran for messenger of her class. One way or another it seemed she had to make the children choose her.

> Vote for Peg
> Of thee I beg

How hopefully, how fearfully she magic-markered her campaign posters, her mouth forming the letters as painstakingly as her fingers.

> Shake a leg
> And vote for Peg

And how confidently she ran off to school on election day morning. "I've got it made, mother. I mean I know I'd never get president, but all the good kids have already been something and only Bobby Pierce and Frank Giavani are campaigning against me for messenger, and they're the worst boys in the class. I know none of the girls will vote for them, and the boys' vote will be split."

Personally, I wanted messenger for her so badly I was afraid to hope.

And indeed she sang a different tune as she huddled in my lap that afternoon, awkward ten-year-old legs dangling between the slats on the back of our Boston rocker. "We made speeches on why we wanted to be messenger. Frank Giavani got a lot of clappings for his speech, and I hardly got any clappings. And *Frank Giavani* got messenger. Why, mama? Why didn't I get any clappings?"

Because the other children like you even less than they like the worst boys in the class, I answered, though only in the deadness of my heart. Oh, Peggie. Peggie.

Then in the sixth grade the climax came. Not anything big. Just that Peggie finally put her *separateness* into words. How forlorn she looked standing there dry-eyed in the middle of the kitchen floor, her unguarded schoolgirl body heaving convulsively. "I wish *I* had a friend," she said finally. "I mean Jody has Kim and Dawn has Cathy and Nancy has Mary Ann, but I don't have anybody."

I didn't know whether to put my arms around her or not. I didn't know what to do really. But in the end I said what seemed the only thing to say, "Well, honey, let's pray about it." Of course I'd prayed about it all through the years, but this right-out-in-the-open praying *with* Peggie was something new for me. "We're just going to pray," I declared, "that God will give you a friend."

And so we did.

It wasn't long, just a few days, before a very different girl came bouncing in from school. "You'll never guess what happened today," she began. "Miss Murdock changed our seats and I sit next to Heidi now and Heidi *has asthma.*"

I looked at Peggie blankly.

"Now you may not know this, mother, but asthma is a lot like cystic fibrosis. How many times have I been in the hospital? Three times, right? Do you know how many times Heidi's been in the hospital? Three times! And Babies and Childrens, mother. The same hospital. She even had the same doctors. And she slept in a tent and they did therapy on her just like on me and when I talk about cystic fibrosis she knows what I'm talkin' about."

"Well, that's very — "

"See that white house over there with the back porch?" Peggie asked, dragging me over to the kitchen window. "That's Heidi's house. In the summer we can wade right through the creek to see each other. Isn't it funny — she was right there all this time and we never knew?"

"Well, I'm not so — "

"And she works in the school library, mother. And I kept asking her about it and finally she said, 'Would you like to work in the library too, Peggie?' And I said, 'Yes.' "

"My goodness," I commented meaningfully, "she likes books, too? That is a lot of coincidences." I didn't want to preach, but I wanted to make sure Peggie realized from *whence* this great gift had come. And then I had to turn away to hide the tears that suddenly steamed to the surface from some hot well of feeling way down inside.

It seemed I had to turn away often after that, but the tears were mostly tears of relief and gratitude as Peggie continued to bound in from school with her up-beat comments.

> I was sittin' with these girls at lunch today, mother. You know, the four of us who kind of make a group? And they were all tellin' beer stories, and I said I drank root beer. Oh, mother, isn't that the funniest thing?

> When I went back to school today I still had the hospital bracelet on my arm, and all the kids came crowdin' around. I mean I couldn't move. And they were all sayin', *How are you, Peggie? It's good to see you, Peggie.* And even the boys, mother, the boys were sayin', *Glad you're back, Peggie.*

> We had elections today, mother. In the sixth grade you do it different, and everybody who wanted to be anything went out in the hall and they kept voting and you kept getting eliminated, and finally I was the only one left and I got it, mother. I got it. I got *president!*

"I got them, mother. I got them." It took me a moment to realize that Peggie's voice was coming to me not from the past, but through the window of the car, and that what she'd gotten this time was not the presidency of her class but Heidi's earrings.

"It took a long time because they had Oreo cookies with one bite gone and strawberry ice cream cones as well as the apple cores, but I finally got the apple cores."

"Well, hop in. I'll have to take you home to wrap them and then back to the post office."

Peggie looked at me with amazement, and then comprehension lighted her face. "I know why you're being so nice to me. It's because the earrings are for Heidi, and you're so glad God gave me Heidi."

You'll never know how glad, honey, I thought. For what a difference it had made to her to have a friend with a problem similar to hers. Somehow it had helped her accept herself, and as soon as she'd accepted herself the other children had accepted her, too. It had never dawned on me that she needed a friend-with-asthma, but God understood her a lot better than I did.

"I'll bet you were sittin' here thinkin' about Joey and C.F. camp, too, weren't you, mother? I know you always say God works for us when we work for ourselves, but I think sometimes when you want something and you can't do anything about it yourself and you want it real bad, He just gives it to you."

"Are you talking about the year Joey got that fever every three weeks like clockwork?"

"Yeah, and he had to go to the hospital every time he got it, and then just before time for C.F. camp he got it again and we prayed he'd be able to go, and the day before camp started the fever went away all by itself."

"It did seem like God worked that out, didn't it?" I asked, feeling again the heat of Joey's body as I'd greeted him on the closing day of camp.

"I'm hot," he'd complained. And by the time we'd gotten him home he'd been burning up. But he'd had a glorious, fever-free week at camp.

"Well, you know, mother, C.F. camp is the only place in the whole world where you're normal if you have C.F. I mean if a kid walked in that camp who didn't have C.F., he'd feel odd. Now I think it's real neat to have a God who cares about stuff like that.

"Including even little bratty brothers," she added playfully.

"If Joey heard you say that, he'd say, 'Including even big bratty-without-the-b sisters.' " We laughed together. But how right he'd be, I thought. It really was neat to have a God who cared about eleven-year-old girls who needed best friends.

"Including," Peggie piped, "even old, old bratty-without-the-r mothers and fath — Help! Anybody at all out there! Help!"

Conversation About Being Different

"Somebody Always Says
I Have Skinny Arms"

Conversation About Being Different

"What'll I wear today, mom?" Joey asked, slurping away on his Grape Nuts.

"Same thing you wore yesterday."

"What should I wear today, mother?"

A certain edge sounded in Peggie's voice, and I groaned inwardly, knowing she'd keep at me till I made a suggestion and then oppose any suggestion I made. "How about your sailor pants and red top?" I ventured bravely.

"Oh, mother, *that*? I like things with long sleeves. I mean, every time I wear that top somebody always says I have skinny arms."

"Yeah, mom. How come I'm this big around," Joey put in, forming his fingers into a tiny circle the size of his wrists, "and everybody else in my class is *this big* around?"

"Well, that's a part of having cystic fibrosis. Look at the other children in the doctor's office sometime. Almost all of them are thin."

"Oh yeah? Well, I'm not thin here," he said, pointing to

53

his potbelly. Actually, with his emaciated arms and legs and distended stomach he looked like something out of a concentration camp, but he strutted off patting his now fuller than usual middle, smiling contentedly.

"Now that," I said to Peggie, "is what I call well-adjusted."

"Meaning?" she demanded, perching herself on the edge of the table as was her custom in the mornings when Joey went off to dress. The two got up and had breakfast together, but Joey left for school earlier than Peg. Usually we had a good talk time as she sat there, legs swinging happily, and I flitted about cleaning up the kitchen. Something told me this was not going to be one of those good mornings.

"Meaning," I said calmly, "that Joey's aware of the ways in which he's different from other children, but that his basic concept of himself is so good that knowing he's different doesn't keep him from knowing he's still a pretty nice guy."

"Meaning I'm not well-adjusted?"

"Well — let's just say you're more the creative type. You know, I read something in *Reader's Digest* the other day I've been wanting to show you. Wait a minute and I'll find it." I went over to the pile of magazines on the teacart and leafed through them, looking for the one with the Pearl Buck quote and finding it finally in the June issue.

> The truly creative mind in any field is no more than this: a human creature born abnormally, inhumanly sensitive. To him a touch is a blow, a sound is a noise, a misfortune is a tragedy, a joy is an ecstasy, a friend is a lover, a lover is a god, and failure is death.

"You mean things bug me more than most kids?"

"Do you realize that in the past week alone you've bemoaned skinny arms, flabby legs, ugly feet, hair with no body, bags under your eyes, and pimples under your bangs?"

Peggie bristled, but a moment later broke down and giggled. "I don't really mind all those things that much, except maybe my skinny arms."

"Actually I understand something about the way you feel," I said kindly. "I've always been self-conscious about being two sizes bigger on the bottom than the top. I think the reason I like long dresses so much is that I'm convinced the more of me I cover up the better."

"I didn't know *you* felt like that. Really, mother?" Peggie looked me over furtively. "Two sizes you say?" She tittered behind her hand. "On the bottom?"

"You enjoyed doing that, didn't you?"

"Now, mother, don't go tellin' me the reason other kids make fun of me is because they have problems. They told us all that stuff last year, and it didn't help a bit. Anyway some kids don't have any problems, like you just said with Joey."

"I didn't say Joey doesn't have any problems," I replied, "just that most of the time he doesn't let his problems make him feel he isn't any good."

I pushed the toast crusts down the drain, and then while the disposal roared I thought about how a few nights before Joey had come downstairs way after bedtime and curled up in my lap. Finally it had come out that the boys in his class were calling him "little guy," and that day when he'd been walking home from school they'd shouted, "Move out, little guy," and pushed him off the sidewalk. Just telling me had made him cry. "I hate it when they shout that," he'd said. *"Move out, little guy."*

I told Peggie about this now, and she looked at me with an expression of disbelief. "I didn't think anything bothered him," she said.

"Everybody has something that bothers them," I told her, "and everybody's much more concerned with how they look to you than with how you look to them."

"Yeah, but it's worse with my C.F. Last year I weighed sixty-three. Mother, I looked like a skeleton. And this boy on the bus always says, 'Here's the kid with the black teeth.'"

"Hair without body, bags under your eyes, *and* black teeth," I said, trying to keep it light.

"And when I wear my poodle skirt they ask me if I'm

pregnant. *And* when I cough they all cough with me." Just thinking about coughing got her started right then, and she coughed on and on becoming red in the face and teary-eyed in the process till all at once she was crying for real.

"You know, mother, you think I'm so good and I've improved so much, but when I cough and those girls say 'Cover your swamp' or 'Stop polluting us,' I hate them. Sometimes in school I explode, and I look inside myself and I see so much hate it's scary."

How I hurt for my daughter. In an eyeball to eyeball confrontation she could outstare death. She could see clear through the *thickest* problems of the universe, but she couldn't bear the sight of one square inch of her body that deviated from the norm.

"Don't hate yourself for the hate, honey," I said, standing beside her and gathering her in my arms, my own insides churning. She continued to sob.

I knew it was more than physical oddities that bothered her. For Joey hadn't been the only one with a hurt to share recently at a forbidden time. A few weeks earlier Peg had barged into my study one afternoon when I was writing and squeezed herself down beside me in the big chair. I know I'm not supposed to be here, her attitude said, but isn't this nice and cozy?

I had stopped working and looked down at her with a combination of pleasure and exasperation. She'd wept that time, too. "Oh, mother, I just want to be like everybody else," she cried, pressing her face into my shoulder. "But I can't be. I don't want to be different, but I am different." I had no idea what had brought on this outburst, but I said nothing till she had her cry.

"All right now," I said then, "let's talk about this thing reasonably. Just how are you different?"

"Well, it's partly that I have C.F. But it's more than that. It's like how I like to read all summer and everybody else likes to swim. And all the kids wear sloppy jeans and dirty tennis shoes to school. If I dressed like that, I wouldn't feel I had any respect for my school. I just have to dress in a way that shows I respect my school. But all the kids kept callin' me moldy today. I mean they can tell just from lookin' at me I'm a moldy.

"And then in math we have this real old teacher. I mean she's really — how do you say it — senile. And she keeps talkin' about her childhood and all the kids laugh at her right in front of her. And today Joanne said, 'Boy, we've got a weirdo,' right out loud so she could hear. But I like the teacher, mother, and I just can't make fun of her.

"All the kids think the only way to be cool is to act sophisticated and ignore people," she went on, "and if you say anything, say something mean. But I can't be like that. I just have to be cheery and say 'Hi' to kids. But they won't say 'Hi' to me back. Why, mama? I always thought I was a good friend. You know at C.F. camp I got the Best Friend Award and daddy took me aside and told me that one award was worth more than all the awards Joey got."

My heart ached with an old, familiar aching. It wasn't so much that Peg had lost the innings she'd won in the sixth grade. It was more that junior high was a whole new ball game, a game too rough for her to play.

"I don't know what I can say, honey — "

"Well, I'll tell you what you can say. Just say it's awful. That's what you can say."

"I know it's awful. It's just terrible," I said, fighting to maintain my composure, "but don't you think maybe the kids respect you more than they let on?"

"You know how most of the kids the teachers remember are the ones that are especially bad? Well, when I started J.F.K. I made up my mind that the teachers would remember me 'cause I was especially good. You think the kids would respect me if they knew that? They'd think I was crazy. They think I'm crazy anyway. It's like they aren't gonna let anybody be different. They're gonna make everybody be like them."

We had talked for a long time that afternoon. I'd

suggested that Peggie look for other kids who were hurting and do something for them. And that she look at the good things in her life, not just the bad, and thank God for them. But nothing had helped. Not even Romans 8:28.

"How?" she'd snorted at me. "Precisely how is my being different gonna work good for me?"

It didn't look like I was going to have success today either, but I had to try.

"I think one reason you and I are so sensitive to pain," I said, "is that not only do we hurt, but we have a way of standing back and knowing that we hurt. So it hurts double. It goes back to being creative. If you do decide to be a writer someday, that kind of awareness will be one of your biggest assets. You remember that book I've been reading by Malcolm Muggeridge?"

"How could I forget, mother?"

"Well, he has one chapter devoted to sketches of the lives of the people whose writings have meant the most to him. Now he didn't point it out, but I couldn't help noticing that all those people were handicapped in some way. One of them, Soren Kierkegaard, was so deformed that children would run down the street after him pointing and laughing, and if mothers wanted to scare their children they'd say, 'If you don't stop that you'll become a Soren.' But that Soren wrote some of the most beautiful words on Christian love that have ever been written."

Peg sat there stonily, determined it seemed to be unmoved by anything I could say.

"Well, what do you think?" I asked her. "When we stand before God and He evaluates our lives, is He going to say, 'Well done, Miss America. You measure 36-24-36. Enter into the joy of the Lord'?"

That at least got a reaction. "Moth-er!" she cried, scandalized. "I'm gonna tell daddy what you said. He'll get you for that."

"Oh, I'm scared," I stammered, hands fluttering to my face.

And then, "All I'm trying to say is that we'd all be a lot better off if we'd think a little less about how our bodies look to men and a little more about how our souls look to God."

"But you don't know what it's like at John F. Kennedy," Peg protested. "It'd be one against the world."

Probably so, I thought. Probably so. When I was her age the minister always told us we should be different from the world. By which he meant we shouldn't smoke, drink, go to movies, or wear make-up. Of course I'd come to realize since that while the Bible did say we shouldn't love the world, what it meant by world was the whole thought-system of people who lived apart from God's love, like the kids at junior high who thought that what counted was all on the outside. And Peggie might well have to stand alone against it.

I didn't think she needed me to tell her this right now, however. Perhaps I'd been wrong to try to be rational about this thing at all.

"I don't know if this will help or not, honey," I said, "but daddy and I both think you're really special. Not just different from — but better than — the crowd. That's what your differentness makes you in our eyes — super-special."

She jerked herself away from me. "In junior high," she said, "what mothers think doesn't count. And if you get highest honors that doesn't count. And if you're first seat in the band that doesn't count."

"I was reading a psalm yesterday," I said, "in which the psalmist was talking a lot like you. Nobody believed in the things he believed in. Everybody was out to get him. But he referred to himself as 'the apple of God's eye.' Now maybe that's the way you should start thinking about yourself. Of course I can't prove it, but I'd be willing to bet God's up in heaven right now looking down over the whole earth thinking, 'That young girl down there spread out on the kitchen table, is she ever the apple of my eye.'"

Peg was silent again. I had the strong feeling she wanted to tell me God didn't count in junior high either but just didn't dare. I knew it was true, though, that God didn't count very much in junior high. Joe always did maintain that the hardest time in all your life to be a Christian is the time spent in junior and senior high school.

And then Peg looked at the clock. "Sermons! Sermons!" she exploded. "Ask a question and what do you get around here? Sermons! Do you realize, mother, that I still don't know what to wear?"

"Well, if you don't put on something soon," I snapped, my own patience growing thin, "you'll be going to school in your birthday suit, and think what the kids would say about that."

"Moth-er!" Peggie slammed her way out of the room.

I collapsed in one of the kitchen chairs, elbows on the table, head in my hands. "Oh, well, you can't win 'em all," I comforted myself. But even then I knew that one day soon I'd be hearing again at least some of the ideas I'd just expressed, as they emerged directly from the independent mind of Peggie Woodson herself.

Conversation About Mothers
Who Grow Old Before Their Time

"You Always Have A Headache Or You're Tired"

Conversation About Mothers
Who Grow Old Before Their Time

Peggie sat on the couch beside me busy with compass, protractor, and colored pencils. Summer vacation was the time for creating exotic geometric forms for no reason except that you felt like creating exotic geometric forms.

"Did you like Ginger?" she asked at length, referring to a new friend who'd spent the afternoon with her playing Scrabble.

"Mmm-hm," I said absently.

"I like her 'cause she's so peppy. Did you think she was peppy?"

"Mmm-hm."

"It runs in her family," Peggie said significantly. "I mean if you think Ginger's peppy, you should see her mom. You wouldn't believe how lively she is. You know I been wondering, mother, why you're always so tired. I mean you almost always have a headache or you're tired. How come?"

"Wait a minute, honey. I'm right at an interesting part," I said, holding up my *Screwtape Letters*. And actually I was at an interesting part, but I'd have had to keep Peg at bay regardless.

For I couldn't very well tell her the obvious "how come."

I couldn't very well tell her I was tired from keeping an eight-room, three-bath parsonage dust-free in order to keep her and Joey's lungs dust-free. Or from hours spent draining the mucus from their lungs, mixing tent solution, and sterilizing medical equipment. Or from buying and preparing the enormous amounts of food they continually consumed. Or from seeing that eighty-six-and-one-half pills really did go down proper gullets at proper intervals every day.

Nor could I tell her I was tired from doing many of the tasks a father ordinarily does around the house. Tasks her father couldn't do because he was holding down two jobs to cover medical expenses. Or tired from doing many of the jobs children ordinarily perform because she and Joey needed time to relax between the rounds of therapy that put such a strain on their schedules.

What could I tell her? I waved a little s.o.s. prayer heavenward.

"I think partly because I'm just so dumb that I worry all the time," I said. I'd seen my anxiety reflected in the pinched look on Peggie's face lately and thought it might help to bring that anxiety out in the open. "Daddy keeps telling me how silly I am to worry when you're doing so well, but somehow I never learn."

Now it was Peg's turn to be engrossed in what she was doing, and just as well because I couldn't elaborate on this aspect of the problem either, though I knew it to be the crucial aspect.

Peggie and Joe had just returned the day before from a week at church camp. A lot of the pressure had been off with just Joey and me at home, and I'd let all nonessentials go — determined to rest and concentrate on enjoying my son. And we'd had a wonderful time, what with our parcheesi tournament moving first in his favor and then in mine and the planning of special dinner treats together. One day we'd splurged and gone to the Pancake House for a late, late breakfast. And another day we'd walked from one end of the shopping mall to the other looking for a copy of *The Lion, The Witch and The Wardrobe.*

Then when we'd found it and gone home, Joey had stood the cushions on the couch in the family room on end, draped Great-aunt Alice's patchwork quilt on top, and crawled inside. "Won't you come in, madam?" he asked, gesturing generously with his protruding head. I quickly slithered in beside him — lest he change his mind — and lay there, back cricking and eyes straining in the darkness as we read C.S. Lewis together. We found a lot of ways to be close that week, a week *filled with awe* for us both.

But an *awful* week, too. There was the time, for example, when I got three doubles in a row and my winning parcheesi man had to go home. Joey laughed and laughed, threw himself on the floor laughing in that way he has, and then all at once began to wheeze, something he'd never done before. "Children with C.F. can't take any complications," I remembered the doctor saying. "A sinus condition, an allergy — a wheeze — any one such thing can tip the balance between life and death." I grew limp remembering how all through the silent maneuvering of the rest of the game that ominous wheezing went on and on.

Then the chicken and the corn-on-the-cob he begged for with shining eyes went almost untouched on his plate. And I knew that when children with cystic fibrosis are doing well, they eat as much as two or three normal childern. When they eat little — well, those untouched drumsticks struck terror to my heart.

Even the sense of unique completion I felt walking through the stores with my male child by my side was splintered by the sight of his birdlike legs sticking out below his shorts. Would I ever be able to shop in that mall again surrounded by other mothers with their male children by their sides if mine was no longer with me?

Perhaps I had more time than usual that week to think about the future, possibly to feel sorry for myself. But any mother whose child has received the *final verdict,* who has carried her appeal to the highest court and been denied, who lives day by day with signs that the date of execution is drawing near — even if those signs are imagined — will understand how I ended my week of rest so exhausted physically and emotionally that for the first time in my life I felt *I* was going to die.

The couch was put back to rights now, and I turned to Peggie as she sat there beside me. "Did I seem especially tired when you came home yesterday?" I asked.

"You sure did, mother. I mean I just walked in the door and you were tellin' me to put away my sleeping bag."

"How do I seem now?"

"I have to admit better. I mean a lot better."

"Well, I went to Communion service this afternoon."

"Sure, mother," Peg said depreciatingly. "You went to Communion, and that little piece of bread they gave you made you feel stronger. Sure. Sure."

"Sure, and you better believe it," I replied. Peggie was just this year studying for church membership and hadn't yet gotten to "The Sacraments." How could I best explain my thoughts to her?

"Okay," I said. "I worry a lot of the time for no good reason. But what about Jesus? Did He have anything to really worry about?"

"Well, He was more like me than you, mother. I mean He knew ahead of time He was gonna die."

How matter-of-fact we'd become about all this as the months wore on — on the surface at least. I couldn't speak for Peggie, but I knew that her nonchalance did something to me deep down inside — something I didn't even care to examine enough to put into words.

"It was six months before the Crucifixion, wasn't it," I asked, "that the Bible says Jesus set His face resolutely toward Jerusalem?"

"Yeah, but He was perfect. I mean everybody's always sayin' we should feel close to Jesus 'cause He went through everything we go through, but way in the back of my mind I'm thinkin', *but it didn't hurt Him so much 'cause He was God* — like even hangin' on the cross."

"Did He say anything on the cross that gives you a hint as to whether or not He really hurt?"

"You mean when He said, 'Oh my God, why did you desert me, Oh my God,' or something like that?"

"Yes, and when He came out of the Garden of Gethsemane He said, 'My soul is so sorrowful I think that I may die.' Now that's pretty sorrowful, don't you think?" I asked, not adding that I'd come to a new feeling of kinship with Jesus at this point in the last few days.

"The way He died, mother. I guess it must have been awful to think about."

Awful beyond our comprehending, I thought. And yet as Joe said so often in his sermons, it was that six-month period when He was thinking about it that was the most productive period in His life. For it was then that He told His most creative stories and then that He worked His most powerful miracles. Children hadn't gotten on His nerves. Why, He wouldn't let His disciples chase them away. Nor did His death-knowledge put any strain on His relationships with His closest associates. Never had they been more lacking in sympathy for Christ's suffering or more consumed with their own status. Yet never had Jesus been more patient with them, never given of Himself more intimately.

"He didn't *want* to die, though, mother," Peggie said.

"No, He didn't. And that's why it's all the more remarkable that while He did have His bad moments, that cross-bearing period was the most straight-backed period of His life."

"But I thought we were talking about you, mother. Are you sure you're not evading the issue?" Peg asked suspiciously.

I fell silent for a moment, wanting desperately to explain what had happened to me that afternoon as I knelt in the sanctuary that had become a kind of trysting place for God and me. For some time I'd been finding it difficult to worship God with the single-mindedness true worship requires in my own church. Loving Joe so deeply, I couldn't see beyond him, even when he stood in the pulpit. So I'd taken to dropping in on a neighborhood church that had Communion service during the week.

This afternoon had found me kneeling there thinking about the very things Peg and I had just been talking about — about Jesus' courage and my cowardice — and praying that I could be just a little like Him. The rays of the late afternoon sun had slanted through the stained-glass windows, flickering on my open prayer book.

> Grant us therefore, gracious Lord, so to eat the flesh of thy dear Son Jesus Christ, and to drink his blood, that our sinful bodies may be made clean by his body, and our souls washed through his most precious blood, and *that we may evermore dwell in him, and he in us.*

And my whole soul was illumined with the page. I rose and knelt at the altar and prayed with renewed hope that as I ate *the body of Christ* and drank *His blood,* I would assimilate Christ's strength into my body, His stability into my spirit.

"Take and eat this in remembrance that Christ died for thee, and feed on Him in thy heart by faith, with thanksgiving," said the priest, and I fed and was thankful.

"No, I'm not evading the issue," I said to Peggie. "Because when I went to Communion this afternoon and took that *little piece of bread,* as you put it, I was taking into myself the very life of Christ. And this particular time I prayed that the aspect of Christ's life God would give me would be His ability to cope."

Comprehension dawned. "It worked!" Peg shrieked.

"It usually does," I said. "And prayer works. And reading the Bible or books about God helps. But for me Communion helps the most." But then that was logical, wasn't it? I thought. For what I needed basically was what Communion was designed to give basically — not more knowledge about the peace and joy of Christ, but the very life of Christ itself united with my life, the very joy and peace of His Spirit merged with my spirit.

"Well, if you've got all this stuff to help you not be tired, how come you mostly are tired?"

I grew almost sick with sadness as Peg's persistence indicated the extent to which my exhaustion affected her.

"Well," I answered, "I think it's partly because while I do have the resources of Christ available, I never avail myself of them completely. I'm not Christ; I'm still human. And when I worry, I'm still going to get tired. But nothing like I would if I didn't have Him. Just think how it would be to live with me if I didn't go to Communion."

"Groa-oan," said Peg.

"Actually, honey, that's the way you have been living with me for the past few weeks. You know I just realized this morning that what with all the vacations and the comings and goings around here I hadn't been to Communion at all. And I've been neglecting prayer, too. It seems I stay so busy with things that seem essential that I neglect the only truly essential thing there is."

Peggie put a clean sheet of paper on her lap and drew a large green square in the middle. Then, to be sure her message wasn't lost on me, she blocked in the letters S-Q-U-A-R-E in large print and handed the paper to me. "I believe, mother, that's a word your generation understands," she said slyly. "Now my generation has a few other choice words I could let you in on if you like."

"No, no, I don't think that will be necessary," I responded politely, and we grinned at each other. Though I was sure no colorful words her classmates might think up could adequately put down a woman so squarely determined as I to neglect her salvation.

Conversation About Dead Bodies

"Yuk! Isn't That Creepy?"

Conversation About Dead Bodies

"You know what Becky says, mother? She says sometimes when she's in bed at night she imagines she's in her coffin instead, but she's also beside her coffin lookin' down in. I mean she's standin' right there lookin' down in at her own dead body. Yuk! Isn't that creepy?"

It was a hot, humid afternoon, and Peg and I had taken over Joey's tiny bedroom, it being the only room in the house with a working air conditioner. I sat at Joey's sea captain desk typing and Peggie lay curled on Joey's Snoopy quilt reading. What prompted her outburst I'll never know — unless possibly it was our conspiratorial takeover of the forbidden property beyond the large STOP sign taped on the front of Joey's door. Was Peg broaching a subject that for her, as for most people, had a KEEP OFF sign attached?

"Why creepy?" I asked.

"Why creepy? Really, mother!"

"Well, what's so creepy about a house someone's just moved out of?"

Peggie gave me one of her *I should have known she'd say
something like that* looks and prepared to return to *The Fellowship
of the Ring*.

"Actually, honey, I know what you mean," I put in
quickly. "I read once about some missionaries who lost five of
their children on the mission field. One by one they added to the
tiny mounds on a lonely Chinese hillside. Each time the father
scolded the mother for crying so hard. 'It's only Jane's body,'
he'd say. 'Jane's with God.' Or John. Or Phoebe. But the
mother'd say, 'Yes, but that body came out of my own. I fed
that body. And washed that body. When Jane needed comfort,
it was her body I held. All I knew of Jane I knew in that body.'
And in the end she hated her husband."

Peggie sat straight up, spouting indignation. "I know
daddy would never say anything like that missionary. I mean
he's a Christian minister and all that, but he has human feelings
too."

We sat for awhile in silence then, shut in from the world
by the hum of the air conditioner and drawn close to each other
by the coziness of the room as well as our collusion in crime.

"You know what else Becky says, mother? She says her
mom thinks it's gonna be real neat to be without her *pounds of
flesh,* that her mom intends to have a great time zappin' herself
all over the place."

Another silence.

"It's hard to put both sides together, isn't it, mother? I
mean it'd be nice not to have to worry about your body, but it's
been fun trying to make it pretty, too."

How simply and clearly she summarized both sides of the
problem from her thirteen-year-old perspective, I thought, a
lump rising in my throat. I tried earnestly in all our talks not to
lead Peg to believe things were going to be less difficult than
they actually would be, and I was glad she wasn't one for easy
rationalizations. For things weren't going to be easy, from her
perspective or from mine.

Peg's death would be a thing of beauty for me, as it would

release her from all the hurts of her young life, hurts of supersensitive soul as well as faulted body. But ugliness is inherent in all decay, is it not? To say nothing of the decay of all-that-was-left-to-you of a child long looked upon, listened to, and fondled with love.

And then Peg jumped up and ran to me, hugging me fiercely. "Now you see, mother. I'm hugging you, right? I'm hugging *you*. But it's your body I'm hugging."

I held Peggie tightly in response. How thin she was. It seemed I couldn't endure her thinness. And suddenly I realized that I had never let myself absorb the substance of my daughter. Regardless of all the *holding* that had gone on between us, I had never let myself truly feel the skin and bones in which dwelled all I knew of Peggie Woodson, the mortal, unenduring part of Peggie Woodson. Strange the insights that come in unguarded moments. How protective of myself I'd been, never letting my arms be truly full lest one day I be unable to bear their emptiness.

Well, I held her now, my face turned away so she'd not see my tears, but my body binding hers to mine. She appeared to sense the difference, clinging to me and crying some herself — in sadness of course, but in happiness, too, I think. Happiness at being fully received as a corporeal as well as a spiritual being — as Peggie Woodson incarnate.

I couldn't seem to *handle* her enough. Yet while I knew this brief interruption to our dialogue would have a lasting effect on our relationship, I knew also that too much emotion wasn't good for Peg and that I needed to get our contact back on a thinking level.

"We live in such a materialistic society," I said, holding her physically at arm's length. "It's hard to conceive of the soul and the body as two separate entities, isn't it?"

"It sure is," Peg replied, her voice shaking just a little as she joined my effort. "In science we've been studying the brain. The brain you think with, mother, and even it's a part of your body."

And then before I could respond, Joey came racing up the stairs and hurtling through the door. "Out!" he shouted. "Everybody out of my room!"

"Now wait, wait just a minute! Let me ask you a question," Peg broke in, master that she was in the art of distraction. "Are you afraid of dead bodies?"

"Naa."

"Are you afraid to walk alone in the dark in a graveyard at midnight?"

"Yeah."

"Well, if you're not afraid of dead bodies, how come you're scared to walk in a cemetery alone at midnight?"

"I'm ascared to walk anywhere alone at midnight," Joey confessed readily. "Now out! Everybody out of my room!"

"When I was a little girl," I said, "we lived on a busy street without much place to play except a nearby cemetery, and Aunt Lynn and I used to play king and queen there all the time. We'd find a big tombstone for the throne, and Aunt Lynn — being Aunt Lynn — would be the queen and sit on the throne and I'd be the scullery maid and she'd order me about."

"Oh, tell us a real story," Peggie pleaded, "about when you were little."

"Yeah, come on, mom. Tell us a story." I winked surreptitiously at Peg as Joey sat himself cross-legged on the floor and she scrambled down beside him.

"Well, let's see," I said. "How about a story that happened just a couple years ago? A real, sure-enough ghost story?"

Four wide eyes stared at me intently.

"Once upon a time," I began, "there lived a beautiful, forty-two-year-old mother who left her home and traveled far and wide till she came at last to a writer's conference."

My audience giggled and poked each other knowingly.

"Now it so happened that this slender, shapely creature, wearied from her journey, hoped to be assigned quiet quarters of her own. But no sooner had she unpacked her bags than an ordinary looking grandmother, who was really a fairy princess in disguise, was assigned as her roommate.

" 'Would you like to read something I've written?' asked the grandmother.

" 'Not really,' thought the mother, who would have preferred that the grandmother read something *she'd* written. But the mother took the pages offered her and read the story they contained, a true story that enabled her to conquer once and for all a secret fear that had haunted her from childhood.

"And if you guys will stay right here for a minute," I interrupted myself, "I'll run find a copy I have of the story the beautiful mother read and read it to you." I hurried to my study and was soon back rattling the papers in my hand.

"Now," I said, "the name of the story is *No Longer Afraid*, and the name of the author of the story is Grace E. Lorentz, and this is the way it goes.

> It was a cold February morning, just after breakfast. My first grader had gone to school, the two younger boys were playing in the living room, and my husband who had worked for eighteen hours had gone to bed. My friend, Mrs. Pierce, was doing our breakfast dishes, for I had just come home from the hospital the day before, having lost our fourth child.
>
> Sitting on a chair talking to my neighbor, I suddenly realized I was in trouble and needed a doctor quickly. She, too, sensed the situation by my paleness and the look of pain on my face and called my husband.
>
> He came down the stairs two at a time, fastening his clothes as he came, and taking me in his arms, laid me gently on the couch and ran to the corner store to call for an ambulance. It was during the Depression, and we had no phone in the house.
>
> My kindly neighbor stood at my side, deeply concerned.
>
> For a few minutes I felt only extreme weakness and discomfort. But suddenly I was conscious of a great, bright light coming from the corner of the room which I was facing. It was very beautiful and powerful. It reminds me, when I think of it now, of the light depicted in pictures of the Transfiguration.
>
> It drew me toward it, and I felt some part of me lifted from the

body lying on the couch. I could see the body clearly and knew I had left it there, even as somehow I realized I was leaving my children.

From within some consciousness of what was taking place, I lifted my mind to God in prayer. "Oh Lord," I prayed, "please don't take me now for the sake of my children."

As suddenly as it all appeared, it disappeared, and I was back on the couch conscious of my friend standing beside me.

The ambulance came and took me back to the hospital. My doctor was waiting for me at the door of the emergency entrance. He examined me for the vital signs of problems expected in hemorrhaging, and then, with a look of disbelief, he said, "I don't understand it. Your color is good, you have no fever, your pulse is good, and yet you should not even be conscious, or even here. I just don't understand it."

But I understood, and his words only made it all more clear to me. I did still need hospital care and was in there for another two weeks. When I returned home, my neighbor who had stood so faithfully beside me came over to see me.

The first thing she said, after greeting me, was, "You certainly frightened me that day you went to the hospital."

I was anxious to hear why she said this, for I had told no one of that experience — a little afraid of feeling foolish, of being told it was my imagination in a semi-conscious state, I guess. So I calmly asked my friend why, though I didn't feel calm inside.

"Because, I saw you go and come back. I can't explain it, but I know I saw it, and I was so frightened. I am so glad to see you home again," she replied.

It was not my imagination. My neighbor and my doctor confirmed this in my mind.

To me it was a beautiful moment I shall never forget. It is as clear as when it happened. It was that moment when the body is left behind and life goes on in another realm. I was not concerned for my body, just for my children.

No, I am no longer afraid.[1]

---

[1]"No Longer Afraid" used by permission of Grace E. Lorentz, Secone, Pa.

"And, behold, as the mother prepared to hand the papers back to the fairy princess, they turned into a magic wand. And the mother found herself able to believe that a human being does indeed live on — thinking and feeling and willing — after the death of the body. And she overcame forever her morbid dread of corpses, which after all are nothing but the relics of still-thinking, feeling, willing persons.

"And so she returned to her loving, dutiful children and lived happily ever after."

"Wow!" exclaimed Peg. "You roomed with a woman who had that happen to her? My mother, the Celebrity!"

And then Joe came slamming in downstairs. "Where is everybody?"

"Up here in Joey's room," Peggie called. "Temporarily!" And soon Joe's large frame crowded in.

"Not another one," moaned Joey. "Out? Everybody out?" But then he rose to his feet, gesturing dramatically toward his father. "And here, ladies and gentlemen, we have the world's most unusual specimen of a body which must surely, when it no longer has daddy in it, be donated to science."

Joe looked at me questioningly over the children's heads.

"Can you read us something out of the Bible so we won't be afraid of dead bodies?" Peggie asked, and I nodded at Joe encouragingly.

"Well, let's see." Joe took his New Testament from his breast pocket and leafed through it.

In that brief moment I thought back to another encounter I'd had at that same writer's conference, an encounter with an ancient, pink-scalped man with whom I *happened* to share the back seat of the airport limousine. He told me how his wife of fifty years had died and how he'd been inconsolable in his grief until an angel had appeared to him.

"Why are you spending so much time at the cemetery?" the angel had asked. "Nellie isn't there."

I thought, too, of an article I *happened* to read shortly after I returned from the conference, the story of a mother who had seen a supernatural light shining in the funeral parlor above the casket of her son. A supernatural voice had spoken from the light. "He is not here," the voice had said. "He is with Me."

It had been a special period in my life, a period in which God had obviously been trying to free me from my aversion not only to the notion of death, but to all of its mechanics as well.

I said a little prayer now that Joe would be able to make this afternoon equally special for Peg and Joey.

"How about this?" he asked, bending his testament open to the fifth chapter of 2 Corinthians:

> For we know that when this tent we live in now is taken down — when we die and leave these bodies — we will have wonderful new bodies in heaven, homes that will be ours forevermore, made for us by God himself. . . . How weary we grow of our present bodies. That is why we look forward eagerly to the day when we shall have heavenly bodies which we shall put on like new clothes. . . . These earthly bodies make us groan and sigh, but we wouldn't like to think of dying and having no bodies at all. We want to slip into our new bodies, so that these dying bodies will, as it were, be swallowed up by everlasting life (1-4, *Living Bible*).

Peg glanced at me quickly and then dropped her eyes, almost as though it was too much for her. "Hey, that's neat," she said at length. And then, "You know in social studies we've been studying the high cost of funerals. Did you guys realize relatives will pay $75.00 to have a dead person's hair rolled up? I mean it's not every beauty operator that's gonna work on a dead person. Now that's silly. I'm not sayin' you should shave 'em bald or anything like that, but I bet those relatives don't know much about new bodies or they wouldn't spend so much money on the old ones."

Joe put his arm around Peggie's shoulders, and she sidled up to him companionably. "I had a funeral last week, and the funeral director showed me his latest model casket," he told her. "It had gold hinges guaranteed to last fifty years."

At that Joey went rummaging wildly in his closet, emerging with a feathered red, green, and yellow tomahawk he'd picked up on some sightseeing tour.

"What's that for?" Peg demanded.

"To dig!" he cried. "To dig for them thar gold hinges!"

Had we really accomplished anything, I wondered. Could I hope to have accomplished anything in one hour to offset the deeply ingrained feeling of "creepiness" with which Americans view corpses and caskets and dirgeful burials — if ever they do view them, if ever they do drag them out of the mind's dark back rooms reserved for the special horrors of life.

And then Joey raised his tomahawk menacingly at Peggie. "Out!" he yelled, in what was plainly an order whose hour had come. "Oh, I can just see her bloody body now," he gloated, "layin' dead on the battlefield."

Peggie looked at me and shrugged with big-sister contempt. "And what would be so bad about that?" she asked. But I noticed she did get out.

Conversation About Guilt

"I Wanted To Sock Her Right In The Mouth"

Conversation About Guilt

We spread our blanket on the shores of Fire Island, and Joe and Joey raced to the water's edge. It was a matter of male pride. They could do nothing on the first day at Fire Island before they built a sand castle, larger and more impregnable than any they'd built the year before.

Peg and I strolled up the beach, feet splashing in the numbing waters, faces raised to the browning sun. We hadn't had much time to be alone recently, what with all the togetherness in New York grandmother and grandfather's tiny house, and I sensed from Peg's willingness to walk away from the castle building that she wanted to talk to me privately. It didn't take her long to start.

"You know what that Cassandra said to me the other day?" she blurted with unusual belligerence. "She said the reason I have C.F. is that I don't have enough faith — that God would heal me if I didn't have the tiniest bit of doubt in my mind that He would. And all these vacations I been goin' up the street to play with her I didn't even know she was religious. I mean I

wanted to sock her right in the mouth."

"My goodness. Why did you want to do that?"

"Because she's so dumb, mother. Don't you get mad at people who are dumb?"

"Not usually," I said. "But I do get upset with people who make me feel guilty." People, I thought, whose *superior wisdom* makes me responsible for all the calamity in the lives of those I love.

"But you wouldn't believe how dumb Cassie is, mother. I mean she insists that God protects good people, like Daniel in the lions' den, and if something bad happens to you, God's punishing you for your sins." Evidently Cassie's words had been boiling inside Peggie during the brief time they'd been bottled up there, and now they blasted their way to the surface.

"Are you really all this upset, Peg," I asked gently, "just because you think Cassandra's dumb?"

She stood very still then, almost as though she were bracing herself for some force she feared would knock her off balance, her feet sinking deeper and deeper into the surging sand. "It's not true what Cassie says, is it, mama?" she asked, her voice small.

I knew I could give her an emphatic *No!* and temporarily end the discussion. But I knew just as surely that no *No!* of mine would end the debate in Peggie's mind.

"You remember how it was when you were little?" I asked. "If you used the potty, you got a lollipop. If you didn't eat your carrots, you didn't get dessert. Good things happened when you were good and bad things when you were bad. Even now if you get a good report card, daddy takes you out. Right?"

Peggie gave me a puzzled look and fell silent again. "You remember when Mr. Madison died with his liver?" she asked finally. "Well, I heard some people talkin', and they said he drank himself to death. That he had no one to blame — but himself."

Peggie's voice shook on those last words. In fact I could feel her shaking all over beside me, and I led her out of the water and up to a little hollow in the sand. We sat down together, and she leaned up against me, letting my body support her weight. How I wished I could shelter her as easily from the storms of self-blame raging within as from the wind without.

"So okay," I said, "in some cases misfortune is a punishment from God for our sins. The Bible does say, 'Whom the Lord loves He chastens.' And in other cases it's an inevitable result of our sin. We might as well face these facts. But then we have to ask ourselves if it's also a fact: one, that all people are responsible for all the tragedy in their lives; and two, that you're to blame for having C.F."

"If anyone's guilty for me having C.F.," Peg declared, "it'd be you and daddy. I mean you guys had the genes. And I don't mean blue jeans," she added, shoving me with her shoulder in a brief return to her normal good humor. "But know-it-alls like Cassie, they don't listen to stuff like that."

Then the wind carried Joe's voice our way. "Hey, where's our tunnel expert?" he shouted.

And Peg ran off like the wind itself. But I could tell she didn't run away from her thoughts from the words she flung over her shoulder. "I can't stand people who don't have logic."

I wandered up the beach a bit further. Not too far, though, for I didn't want to be out of earshot when it came time for the Queen Mother to admire her castle, to stand in its ankle-deep shelter and declare her safety from the elements. What a carefree beginning of a day it had been, I thought. God's whole expanse of early morning beach inhabited only by the sea gulls, the Woodsons, and the stately rows of trash baskets.

But now all the Cassies of the world marched toward me from every direction, jangling their chains of defeat and depression. How hard I'd tried to protect Peggie from this sort of thing. She was too young to know such deep despair.

It was more than the guilty, wholly guilty, nothing but guilty complex of the society in which we lived. One could, if one must, survive the Cassandras who heaped on us all a corporate guilt for the varied ills of the world. But when they invaded the church of Christ, how lonely they left you.

"You're not believing hard enough," they'd say. "It can't

be God's will for anyone to be sick. You must claim God's promise of healing. Did Jesus ever turn away anyone who asked for healing when He was on earth? Well, He's just the same today."

How simple they made it sound. But when you went that route and nothing happened, they changed their tune. "You're trying too hard," they'd say. "You must relinquish your loved one. Give him up if you want God to heal him."

Whatever you did, they said it was the wrong thing.

Well, I had come to terms with death. I could watch my children die in slow motion if I must. But I could not be responsible. And in one way or another, to one degree or another, it had to be God's will. I could not live outside His plan for me. I could survive any human rejection, but I could not survive rejection by my God. Just thinking about it again brought back the old, familiar, *going-under* feeling.

And, as so often when these periods of total exhaustion overtook me, I realized how *stiff* I'd been holding myself. How, despite everything I'd said to Peg, way down in my subconscious I'd been thinking, If I could just be good enough, Peggie and Joey would get better.

And then all the Cassies broke rank and pounced on me, winding their chains around my head and pulling tighter, tighter. And the pounding of the surf somehow got right inside my skull. "Chargeable!" it pounded. "Criminal!"

In the end, of course, I knew I had to remain calm. I couldn't get a migraine on the first day of vacation. Peggie was right. One had to be logical about these things. More than I needed any other knowledge right now, I needed to know, and on a rational basis, whether or not it would be my fault if my children died. I settled myself down again in the sand. I would establish that knowledge.

Well, it was a matter of record was it not, I asked myself for starters, that good people suffer? What a silly question really. One had only to look at the disciples. Now who had been holier than they? Yet how had they ended up? Beheaded, boiled in oil, skinned alive, crucified upside down. What a gruesome array.

And what about the best person who ever lived? No, what about the only perfect person? Hadn't He ended up on a cross? And hadn't He insisted that any of us who wanted to follow Him had to do just that — follow Him — crosses on our backs? Backs on our crosses?

How would He have responded in His Gethsemane if someone had said to Him, "It could never be the will of Your Father in heaven that His Son should suffer. You insult God when you ask Him to remove this cup if it is His will. You must claim His promise of deliverance. Then believe the cup has been removed. Rise to your feet and act as though it has been removed."

What a forlorn figure He would have been, hanging on that futile cross, encased in a vicious sadness, destroyed in His inmost being by the blood on His own hands.

I began to relax a little and lay back in the sand, my sun hat over my face. I would do what I had told Peggie to do — face things squarely. I would remember as many of the New Testament healing stories as I could, examining each one honestly to see to what extent the degree of each person's faith was responsible for his healing.

I remembered first the woman who had had a hemorrhage for years and who, as she touched the hem of Jesus' robe, knew she would be healed. I guess I thought of her first because hers was the experience I was usually called upon to reproduce. But as I thought on, I found her kind of faith to be the exception rather than the rule.

I found, for example, that even the centurion whom Jesus commended so highly for his faith — the centurion who said, "You need not come — You need only say the word"; the centurion who was used to issuing orders — even this centurion had no thought of issuing orders to Jesus. He put in his request but realized that whether or not Jesus acted upon it was, as with any man of authority, entirely up to Him — the Man of All Authority.

And once a leper came to Christ and actually uttered the forbidden phrase, *If You will* — "If You will, You can make me clean." And Jesus said, "I will. Be clean."

And the greatest healing miracle of all — if it can be called such — the raising of Lazarus from the dead, was certainly not performed because Lazarus or Mary or Martha believed it was going to be. Why even Jesus' most efficient prompting could not induce Martha to entertain the possibility of resurrection.

It was true, I admitted, that in Nazareth Jesus could do no mighty works because of the people's unbelief. But it was in His person they did not believe — in His power basically. I could remember no incident in the New Testament when Jesus refused to heal because the sick person did not know with certainty that he would be healed.

And truly, I thought with inestimable relief, He is just the same today.

I could recall no evidence anywhere in the New Testament of healing on demand. Scoffers at the cross demanded that Christ prove Himself. But no believer ever dared approach Him and say, "You promised. Okay, You produce." Often it seemed people just stood along the roadside hoping. "Have mercy," they cried with outstretched arms. "Mercy."

I was feeling really good. It hadn't been so hard to face things. Why hadn't I done it years ago? I was free somehow. I was not at fault for my children's illness. I was free from guilt. I rose to my feet and with a mighty flourish banished each of the endless number of Cassandras to her respective trash can.

And was ready just in time to do my Queen Mother thing.

And then Joe and Joey went off to look for shells while Peg and I plopped down on the blanket.

"I was telling daddy what Cassie said," she told me excitedly, "and just then this big wave came and we were all bending over and it *rained* all over on top of us and right then daddy said he didn't care what Cassie said 'cause the Bible said the rain fell on the just and the unjust alike.

"Oh, mother, wasn't that neat? I was just standin' there admiring him, and he got this look on his face like when he's tryin' not to be proud but he knows he's gonna say something smart, and he said he didn't care what Cassie said double because even Jesus told the story about the house built on the *sand* and the house built on the *rock* and even Jesus said the same storm hit both houses.

"You know what I'm gonna ask that Cassandra, mother? I'm gonna ask her suppose me and her both built castles on the beach and a big wave came, would it only wash away my castle? Now what are you laughing at?"

"Because you have that same *am I not clever* look on your face that your father gets," I said. "And actually, Peg, that was a clever idea. The only thing is that Jesus said when we believe in Him we're like people who build their houses on rocks. So our houses won't fall when the storms come. That's one thing we can be sure is God's will — that whatever big wave comes crashing down on us, He wants us to stand tall and sure."

"Yeah," Peg said, "that's good. Now that's the way I think. But the way Cassandra talks, you can just order God around — like tell Him what His will is. And that can't be so because then what would all that great intellectual brain of His be for? He wouldn't have nothin' to do with it. No way to use it. You know how Americans like to think they're so smart and high class, smarter than any other people or form of life. Now God would have to be ten times smarter, more than ten times smarter than us, 'cause He invented us. You remember all the animals at the zoo the other day? You remember the orangutans? Well, He thought up the orangutans. I mean if He's so smart, we ought to accept that He knows what He's doing. We're dumb next to Him. I mean the little kids in the nursery think I know it all. They just trust their mommies. But people like Cassandra won't admit they're overemphasizing some points. Her way you could say, *Give me a bike, God. I believe You're gonna gimme a bike,* and He'd have to give it to you. Now I think I do have faith. I think I have faith that God will do what He wants. Am I talkin' too much?"

"No, honey," I said and just couldn't help that the words came from my throat as half-laugh, half-sob. "You're not talking too much. In fact, I hope you never stop talking like you're talking now. I doubt that anyone else has ever made quite such a good statement of faith as you've just made — certainly not as original. So if any more sassy Cassies come into your life, I'll line up behind you and deliver a punch of my own." She didn't think I meant it, but she enjoyed even my pretend vehemence on her behalf.

And, of course, I didn't mean it. If any more Cassies came along, I'd go to church and say a special prayer for them. For someday something bad would happen to them, too, and no amount of believing would make it go away. And, oh, the desolation they would feel.

Yes, I'd kneel in prayer for them and for myself. My head would be bowed and my knees bent before God, my Creator, but my back would be straight as one of God's creatures. And I knew that was the way He wanted me to be.

Conversation About Mothers Who Get Angry

"I Love You, Mother, And
I Hope You Love Me Too"

Conversation About Mothers Who Get Angry

"I wonder if you realize, Peggie," I said in voice ominously calm, "that in the past two days we've looked in twelve different departments of five different stores for one lone top, one ordinary top to go with one pair of ordinary jeans, and that the only thing we have to show for our effort is *one small tube of acne cream*." I threw the bag on the kitchen counter in a splash of indignation.

"I wish to inform you, mother, that when I went shopping with grandmother I found a lot of things I liked." The words could have been impertinent, but Peggie's voice was patient. She recognized the storm signals and was simply listing a fact she hoped would offer shelter.

"You won't look at anything that's not a bright color. You're too big for the girls' department but not big enough in the right places for the junior department. You won't look at anything that doesn't button up to your chin."

"But I can't help it that I don't have a figure. And my neck's so bony."

"You won't look at anything that doesn't have long sleeves."

"But, mother, you know that's because of my skinny arms." Peg's voice squeaked betrayal.

"You don't like anything made of jersey. You don't like anything that's not soft. You won't wear anything that's tight. You won't wear anything that's loose. You won't wear anything that everybody else isn't wearing. You won't wear anything that anybody else you know is wearing." My thunder clapped on and on.

"Well, if I'm as picky as you say about my clothes, how come I have a whole closet full? You have to admit I do have a lot of clothes." I could see it took all her strength to stand and face me, shaking as she was before the violence of my condemnation.

And then the storm broke in earnest. "And how many of those clothes do you wear?" I raged. "How many of the clothes grandmother bought you will you ever put on your back? The next time you want something from the store, you can jolly well get it yourself. You needn't expect that under any circumstances I will ever go shopping with you again. Does it never occur to you that I'd like some new clothes myself once in a while? Don't you care that I get tired? You're a selfish, thoughtless child, never thinking of anybody but yourself."

"But I thought — you always told me — I had an especially — generous heart." Peggie's own emotion rained in gentle flow down her battered face, and she ran from the room and up the stairs.

I leaned against the refrigerator, pressing my cheek to its smooth, enamel side. It was the coolest spot I'd felt all day. The temperature had been in the nineties for a week. Two men had yelled at me out of their car windows as I drove the short distance home from Sears. One of the air conditioners on which the children's health depended was dripping water all over the mantle in the family room. Both their ultrasonic nebulizers were flatly refusing to nebulize, and one air compressor screeched its own protest in strident, clanging tones.

For three sticky months Peg had clung to me, insisting I be mother, nurse, and friend. It had been a long summer. Tomorrow was the first day of school. It hadn't come soon enough.

I moved about reluctantly, putting the spaghetti on to heat and crying a little as I did so. I suppose it was my own tears as well as the sound of Peggie's sobbing at the top of the stairs that brought back a couple tear-drenched incidents of recent weeks.

There'd been C.F. camp, for example. Always a high point in Peggie's life, but this year a low, low valley.

"Joey won an electric Snoopy toothbrush," she moaned at us in greeting on the last day of camp. "We had 'Let's Make A Deal' night, and I dressed up as a head of lettuce and kept waving my sign that said *Lettuce make a deal* and every other girl in camp got called and I never got called once and Joey got called and called till finally he won the grand prize.

"And then we had Olympics night, and Joey won an Olympic shirt and every girl in my cabin got an Olympic shirt and I came in last in everything."

I was sure Peg was exaggerating, yet my heart sank as we went in for the awards program and they kept calling *Joey Woodson for Best in Crafts, Joey Woodson for Most This, Joey Woodson for Most That.* They did call Peggie once, but we knew and she knew the camp arranged for everybody to be called once.

"You see, mother. You see," she whispered. "Everybody notices Joey, but nobody notices me."

We walked through the campgrounds together then, Peg and I, as Joe loaded the car. "You know I been thinkin'," she said, "the only reason I'll come back to camp next year is to be with Patti. I mean all the girls in my cabin got boy crazy since last year, and they all paired off with boys all week. It was so dumb. Three nights I cried myself to sleep I was so lonesome. I wouldn't have had any fun at all if it hadn't been for Patti.

"You know, mother, the reason Patti was vomiting all the time was because she was so upset. I mean she had this real good

97

friend, Jo, she roomed with in the hospital, and they arranged to meet at camp and when Patti got here she looked all over for Jo and she couldn't find her and she was askin' everybody, 'Where's Jo?' And finally the nurse said 'Jo died.' Patti cried all week over Jo. And she was vomiting blood all the time."

"She does seem awfully tired to me."

"Well, she is, mother. She didn't do anything all week because she didn't have any energy. But she has this infection in her lungs, and she's taking medication from Australia and as soon as her infection goes away she'll be all right. I mean the reason she didn't go swimming was because her bathing suit straps were tight, and that's why it hurt her to breathe."

Peg had looked at me, daring me to deny that Patti would be all right. But her face had cracked, and a few angry tears trickled through her tight defenses. We'd both been silent then. There seemed nothing more to say.

There was silence now on the upper landing.

"You give me twice as much trouble as Joey does," I howled up at her. "How many other girls do you think wear their mothers out like this? The least you can do is come down here and set this table. And see if you can do it right for once." I couldn't believe the force of my own cruelty. I knew I was laying waste my own spirit as well as Peg's, yet the currents that had surged silently inside me for so long would not be denied.

As Peg walked into the kitchen, I walked into the living room. I just sat there listening to the sounds of a table being set and thinking nothing until those sounds carried me back to the snack shop where we'd stopped for Peg to buy a root beer float in the middle of yesterday's shopping trip. The cigarette smoke from the next table had drifted our way, and Peg had gone off into an endless fit of coughing. The small restaurant, full of jabbering school kids, had grown uncannily silent as every pair of eyes had turned to stare at her.

"Now that's what I keep tellin' you, mother," Peg groaned. "That's what it's like at school. Can you imagine when you're having a test or something? You know what I'm known as? The girl with a thousand and one diseases. I mean this perfectly strange kid walked up to me one day and said, 'Are you the girl that's dying of a thousand and one diseases?' When I had gym, whenever I tried to do anything I'd start to cough and all the kids would back away and nobody'd be my partner.

"I don't suppose I could stay home from school and have a tutor?" she asked, though not too hopefully.

"No, honey, I don't suppose."

"Patti stayed home last year, and the phone company put an intercom in her room and she could hear her teachers and talk back and everything. I don't suppose — "

"I don't suppose."

"And if I get sick, I still have to go, right?"

"Right," I had said, and the answer was still, "Right." I couldn't let Peggie cop out of life.

I slouched further down into the overstuffed living room chair. What an awful time we'd had at the beginning of school last year. Peggie got *sick* every day and lost six pounds the first five weeks of school. And we got sick ourselves following the advice of the psychologist to whom her physician had referred her. "If you vomit," we said, "no matter how hard or how many times, as soon as you stop you go to school."

She stopped getting sick after that, but she hadn't liked school any better. We talked to her about transferring to a parochial school, but she insisted hysterically that "religious kids would be as bad as regular kids." As much as she dreaded known hurts, she feared unknown hazards more. We talked to her school counselor, and he had been the greatest. Excused Peg from gym. Talked to her worst tormentors. Did everything he could to make things easier. And it had helped, though not enough.

And here I was the day before her trial by fire was to start again — adding fuel to the flames. I hated myself for the way I was acting. Knew I'd hate myself for a long time to come for my behavior that day. *But, dear Lord, I try so hard.* I try so hard to make Peggie well, and she just won't get well. Nobody with cystic fibrosis ever gets well. I try so hard to make her happy, but she refuses to be happy.

Peggie had finished setting the table now and walked into the living room, eyes down. And I walked into the kitchen — all the bluster gone out of me. There on my plate I found an envelope I recognized as belonging to Peggie's best "Thank You" stationery. I opened it and read the note she'd written.

> Dear Mama,
>
> Thank you for going shopping with me. I'm sorry I was in such a crummy mood and didn't like anything. I love you, and I hope you love me too.
>
> Love,
Peggie

She came and stood quietly by my side. "I found a note on my plate," I told her. "It was written by a greater person to a much lesser person." Peggie put her arms around me, and we cried together.

"It isn't that I don't love you, honey. Don't ever think that. It's that I do love you. I care so much that when you hurt, I hurt, too, and the hurt grows and I do everything I can to help, but nothing helps and the frustration grows and somehow it all turns to anger. But I'm the one at fault. Not you. Never believe that. No matter what I say. You're the best there is."

Peg hugged me fiercely. "I get mad sometimes, too, you know," she said. "Are we gonna eat soon?"

"Why don't you tell daddy and Joey supper's ready?" I asked.

Then as my hands were busy cutting the French bread and tossing the salad, my mind was busy with one more scene from the past. Peg and her dad had gone camping overnight. It had been a good time marred only by the agony of the little dog tied up at the next campsite. It seemed that its owners had gone off for several hours, and the dog had barked all the time they'd been gone. "Because he loved them so much and he was lonesome," Peggie'd said. Then when his owners had returned the dog had barked all the louder "because he was glad to see them," and his master had picked him up and punched him, "just like a punching bag, back and forth and back and forth," and then dropped him, and the dog had made "awful noises" for a couple minutes and then gone running back to his master.

I knew why this memory had come to my mind at this particular time. I was wondering what had happened to Peggie — why she hadn't stormed back at me as she would have done a year ago. In screaming skill, she was every whit my equal. Whence this growing sweetness? Had I been so awful a mother I'd beaten all the human spirit out of her?

Oh, God, help her, I prayed. Please don't let her cough too much tomorrow. Let her find someone to eat lunch with and ride the bus with. Let somebody tell her they like her new shoes. And if possible, please could she gain a few pounds and could just a little of it settle on her arms —

The family trooped in then, noisy and hungry as usual. Peggie stopped by my chair on the way to hers. "Don't worry about me too much tomorrow, mom," she said, a surprising thing for her to say since I'd made every effort to conceal my concern. "You never can tell. I might have the time of my life." Her voice lilted, but I knew how hard she was reaching — for my sake as well as for her own.

I knew, too, that this child was not being drained of any human spirit, but that her human spirit was being filled with something more. Knew, in one of those brief moments of knowing, that in the forced sparkle of her eyes I was glimpsing specks of the love-light of God Himself.

Conversation About Carrying Your Own Load

"I'm The One With C.F. —
Not You!"

Conversation About Carrying Your Own Load

They were worse even than last year — Peg's first days at school. Worse than anything she or I had feared. How I waited for her to come home each afternoon, watching for the doorknob on the front door to turn, hoping and praying things had been better that day. How I dreaded her return — her tears, her endless accounts of her various ordeals.

You remember that boy, Eugene, that used to say mean things to me in the hall? Well, this year he's *in* my math and *in* my art. I mean I just walked in math today, and he said in this big, loud voice, "Ignore her. She's dying."

And in social studies I had a coughing spell, and I couldn't stop, and the teacher said did I have a cold and did I want to go see the nurse about my bad cough. Oh, mother, she called everybody's attention to it.

And then last period Mr. Allan brought my things to me. I mean I couldn't get my locker open so he kept my things includin' the little folding umbrella I keep in my locker and he walked in and said, "Here's your umbrella, Peggie." And all the

kids were laughin'. And they were sayin', "Why do you have an umbrella, Peggie?" And I didn't know what to say, so I said, "Because my mother makes me," and they said, "Does your mother make you wear 'wubbers' too?"

So greatly did my agitation increase as the days wore on that by Thursday of the second week I was seeing doorknobs turn all day long, and on Friday I fell apart.

"This thing is dominating my whole life," I cried to a friend. "I can't function normally in any area any more. I can live with any other aspect of Peg's having C.F., but I can't take what the kids are doing to her." And how much like Peggie herself I was at this point, I thought. How much like every mother of every child set apart by whatever oddity.

"Maybe you're not supposed to take it," my friend responded thoughtfully. "You're not God, you know. And you're not Peg. If you want my advice, it's *bug off, mother.*"

"Well, thanks so much for your compassion and constructive suggestions."

My friend ignored my sarcasm. "There's a chapter in the Bible," she said, "in Galatians 6, I think, where two separate bits of advice are given a few verses apart on how to handle people with problems. The first, 'Bear one another's burdens' — but the second, 'Each man will have to bear his own load.' "

"Yesterday when Peggie came home," I replied acidly, "she told me how Eugene keeps bringing his friends over and saying, 'Smile, Peggie, and let so-and-so see your black teeth.' Then he uses her teeth to prove she's dying. There were tears in her eyes when she told me. She said, 'It wasn't so bad last year when I didn't know I was dying, but now I know I am.' She's explained a hundred times that her teeth are discolored from antibiotics. She doesn't know what else to do. You want me to turn my back on her? The situation's more than she can handle."

"There's another verse in the Bible," answered my Bible-spouting friend, "in 1 Corinthians 10:13 that says:

> For God keeps his promise, and he will not allow you to be tempted beyond your power to resist; but at the time you are

> tempted he will give you the strength to endure it, and so
> provide you with a way out.

You're going to have to decide if you believe the Bible at this
point, and particularly — after you've done everything you can
for her — if you believe it for Peggie."

With a friend like you, I thought, I could use a few
saber-clutching enemies. But I went and got my Bible com-
mentary and looked up the second of the two verses in Galatians.

> But there is a burden which a man must bear himself. The word
> which Paul uses is the word for a soldier's pack. There is a duty
> which none can do for us and a task for which we are personally
> responsible. There are things which no one, however kind, can
> do for us, and which, however much we want to, we cannot
> push off on to someone else (William Barclay, *Letters to the
> Galatians and Ephesians*).

"Everyone must carry his own load."

But that was for grownups, I argued. Peg was a child. Yet
I couldn't get the words out of my mind, or the advice the
psychologist had given us the year before. "Part of Peggie wants
to run and hide from the situation at school," he'd said.
"Another part wants to stand and fight. You must encourage
the part of her that wants to get on top."

Nor could I forget a comment Joe had made to me a month
or two earlier, a comment that had irritated me ever since. "I
think you encourage Peggie in her poor-mouthing," he'd main-
tained. "She makes things out to be worse than they are when
she's around you."

I'd gotten huffy with Joe, too, of course. Nobody living in
our house should need to be told I was a mother outstanding
both in her sacrifice and her wisdom.

Still, by three-thirty on this particular Friday afternoon I
was ready to approach Peggie from a new direction. "I think,
honey," I would say, "that for a few days you'd better keep the
bad things that happen to you in school to yourself. Not because
I don't care about what happens, but because I care so much I
can't take it for awhile. You know the Bible does say each of us

must carry our own load." Undoubtedly this rejection on top of all her other rejections would bring on a three-day stomach ache at the very least, but then I would have routed my antagonists. And it was true — I couldn't take it any more.

But a strange thing happened when Peg came home that afternoon. She had no complaints.

"I was waiting in the office to see this teacher," she said. "His name was Mr. Brooks, and he didn't know me, and my back was to him and he kept saying, 'You're next, ninth grader,' and I didn't know he was talking to me and finally he came over and tapped my shoulder and said, 'Hey, ninth grader.' He really believed it, mother. He actually thought 'itty bitty me was a ninth grader."

And then a little later, "You know, mother, I've been noticing there are a lot of nice kids at school. I mean the mean kids are still there, but if I don't look at them all the time I see nice kids, too."

As the days went by, Peggie returned to her negative reporting, but it was always interspersed with the positive. And I began to analyze these positive comments. A few were of the Mr. Brooks' variety. The change that was beginning to take place in Peg did result in part from the understanding and kindness of several Mr. Brooks. Might God reward them all. But, basically, we'd been begging God to control the external events in Peggie's life, while He'd chosen to control what was going on inside Peggie instead.

"There's this real popular girl at school," she said one day, for example, "and I never thought she'd want to have anything to do with me. But this morning I summoned up all my courage and I said 'Hi' to her, and her eyes lit up and it was like I could see way down into her soul and she was glad I said 'Hi.' "

And on another occasion, "You know how I eat three times as much as anybody else, mother?"

Oh, I knew all right. We'd suffered together for years over the kids making fun of her appetite.

"Well, you should see me in the lunchroom," she said, a

note of braggadocio in her voice. "All the other kids bring a bag with one little sandwich, and I bring my huge bag and I just dump it all out on the table at once and when I get done with that they give me what they don't want from theirs. I mean today I ate Mary Ann's Twinkies and half of Jody's bologna sandwich, and I'd say, layin' them end to end, approximately fifty centimeters of Carol's pretzels."

The intimacy of God's awareness of what was going on in my little world, the individual way He dealt with our problems, to say nothing of the perfection of His timing, left me feeling cared for beyond all human measure. As, of course, I was. I hadn't been able to take the advice from my friend, or my husband, or even a professional understander of adolescents. But here was God Himself demonstrating for me at the strategic moment that what Peggie needed right now was not another Heidi — not even the silencing of her tormentors, for there would always be Eugenes to poke fun. What she needed right now was to learn to adjust to the fun poked.

I got out my old authority, Dr. Spock, whom I hadn't consulted in years, and read his section on the handicapped child. "As for the stares and pointing and whispered remarks," he wrote, "the child with a noticeable defect has to get used to them, and the younger the easier." How simple it sounded. "If he is hidden most of the week and gets one stare on Sunday, it is more disturbing than ten stares every day, because he is not accustomed to them." God and Dr. Spock, it seemed, were arrayed against me.

Then one day Peggie came home and didn't stop to report to me at all, good events or bad, but raced up the stairs to straighten her room because 'Suzie is coming over to practice,' and I realized the relief I felt at not having her clutch at me was overshadowed by my reluctance not to clutch at her. And I knew I must actively join forces with God's side — and at once. I began the next morning.

"What'll I wear today, mother?"

"Oh, I don't know. Why don't you decide?"

"I don't know what it's like out."

"Well, call the weather and find out."

She dialed the weather, but brought the phone over to where I was doing therapy on Joey. "You listen," she said.

"I can't concentrate on what I'm doing here and that too. You listen."

"It's going to be in the sixties. So what should I wear?"

"Tell you what," I said playfully. "Instead of my telling you what to wear and you telling me why that idea's no good, you make a suggestion and I'll tell you what's wrong with it."

"Well, thanks a lot!" Peggie stomped out of the room.

Soon she was back. "I have to fall down in that dumb play today, so I decided to wear my jeans and shirt. Should I wear my vest too?"

"That's up to you."

"All you have to do is say yes or no."

"Well, that's all you have to do."

She started out of the room again but suddenly whirled around at me, churning with anger and fear. "Why?" she screamed. "Why are you doing this to me? Wait till tomorrow and see what decision I make. You won't believe how ridiculous I'll look. And the first cold day? You just wait. The first freezing day I'll wear my tennis dress!"

They were, of course, only the opening shots in a long, distressing war. My near killing of Peg with kindness hadn't been accomplished in a day. Nor would it be quickly avenged. Oh, we hadn't been as bad as some parents. We hadn't tolerated real tantrums. Peg had some duties around the house. All in all, we were inclined to feel we were raising a beautiful, sensitive human being. Still, I was never unaffected by the hard way she had to go, and the super-sympathy I felt for her moved me to overprotect her, overindulge her — not just in relation to her illness, but in the entirety of her life. Perhaps the very subtlety of my pity had made her addiction to it an even more insidious defeat.

There had been times when she had needed special handling. There would be other such times. But having put my hand to the plow, I would not look back. Her emotional instability did not result from the extent of her physical disability, but from her attitude toward her disability. An attitude which resulted in turn from my attitude. Well, I'd be one handicap with which she'd no longer have to cope. I'd give her just as much support as she needed to stand on her own feet.

"It's not bad enough I perspire so and have to have this short hair and everybody's always thinkin' I'm a boy," she moaned one day. "But this morning we started marching band, and this girl with the cymbals stands next to me and every time she clangs her cymbals every hair on my head stands on end."

"Well, I'd be interested to know how you handled that."

Peggie looked at me out of the corner of her eye and a smile sneaked across her face. "I laughed," she said. "Oh, mother, I couldn't help it. I mean every time the cymbals go *pow,* every strand of my flyaway hair just flies away." We laughed together. In fact every time we looked at each other for the rest of the day, we burst out laughing.

When her accounts of difficult situations persisted, so did my build-up-her-confidence techniques. "I'm sure God let that happen to you and not to me because He knew I couldn't handle it and He knew you could," I'd say. Or, "That was a hard slap. How'd you get the best of that?"

Sometimes she'd yell that I didn't care and she just wouldn't tell me anything any more if I didn't care. And then we'd have a talk about how we have to strike a balance between a dishonest pretending that something doesn't hurt and an equally dishonest encouraging something to hurt more than it has to.

And more and more her interior resources expanded. "I hit Eugene in the stomach with my clarinet case today," she'd say gleefully. Or, "I told those girls if they didn't leave me alone I'd get my father who's a minister to put a jinx on them." That one, it seemed, got the best results. Maybe they weren't solutions I'd have chosen — well, all the better.

For many years I had tried not to worry, tried unsuccessfully to put *my* problems with Peggie into God's hands. But how much easier I found it now to put Peggie and *her* problems into God's hands. And how well He carried them.

"Isn't Eugene bothering you any more?" I asked one day after a long silence on the subject.

"The Eugenes of this world do not change, mother. But you know, I notice he bugs everybody, not just me. And nobody likes him."

"Maybe you should try praying for him."

"Wha-at?"

"Well, an awful lot of people prayed for you at the beginning of this school year and look what's happened to you. Maybe God hasn't taken away your problems, but He sure has made you strong enough to live with them.

"I think it's important that you realize, Peg, that everybody's handicapped in some way. And in my opinion Eugene's handicap is worse than yours. Maybe he lies in bed every night and listens to his parents fight. We don't know. But something terrible must be making him so weak that the only way he can stand up is by knocking somebody else down. Maybe you could begin by asking God to forgive Eugene the way Christ prayed for those who made fun of Him when He was on the cross. Remember? 'Father, forgive them, for they know not what they do.' "

"Oh, but Eugene knows what he's doing, mother. He knows. I mean with him I could say the words, but they wouldn't come from my heart."

"Well, work at it. At the rate you're going, by the time you're finished at J.F.K. there won't be anything you put your mind to that you won't be able to do."

Of course, as much as she continued to improve, there continued to be times when she reverted to old patterns. "These ninth graders were all playing catch with my pills in the lunchroom today," she whined on one such occasion, "and they were sayin' they're gonna report me for takin' dope."

"Oh, honey," I wailed in response. "I'm so sorry you had to put up with that. It's a good thing I can't get my hands on those kids. What kind of young people can they be? You don't know how badly it makes mother feel that you have to go through such things." I admit it. I reverted to old patterns, too — over-fussed, blew the whole thing up.

Peggie didn't like it. She gave me one of her *who do you think you are* looks that I could only interpret as meaning, "Who do you think you are usurping my role?"

"Really, mother," she said in disgust, "do you have to worry right out in front of me? After all, I'm the one with C.F. — not you. I mean, I'm the one who has to live with it."

I was the mother of a child dying, however slowly, of lung disease. Peggie was that child. An altogether different thing. An altogether worse thing. Hers alone was the horror. And hers alone the growing courage. And one day, hers alone would be the glory.

Conversation About Those Left Behind

"God's Nice, Mother. Of Course He'll Take Care Of You"

Conversation About Those Left Behind

Joey was jumping into my arms from four steps up the hall stairs when Peggie rounded the upper landing.

"Am I too big to do that?" she asked wistfully, coming slowly down the stairs.

"Never!" I answered. And she threw herself at me with a wild leap that almost knocked me from my feet, clinging to me with arms twined around my neck, legs locked around my waist, and middle bulging. We stood thus bound, so intent on feeling the form, on absorbing the substance, of each other that it seemed we stood in a segment of infinity.

When Peggie finally scrambled down, she said, "There's nothin' to compare to that, is there? I mean nothin' in the whole world can take the place of that."

I looked at my daughter, loving her as much as any woman has ever loved the product of her womb. Yet as so often was the case when I stood out in the open and let the joy of my love for her swell within me, the pain that always lurked in the shadows came hurtling at me like some giant warrior's lance flung with

117

consummate skill. Always it met its mark, piercing the tender swelling, probing stubbornly.

"I only know one thing that's any better," I told her as Joey strolled off and she and I sat down on the bottom step.

"You mean when daddy puts his arms around you?" she asked, assuming her newly acquired, worldly wise attitude toward sex and poking me slyly in the ribs with her bony elbow.

"Well, that of course," I said, poking her back. "But actually, I was thinking about God."

"You mean God hugs you?"

"Yes, quite often now."

"Is it a feeling?"

"Well, it's a feeling and a thinking. It's peace and joy and love and hope all mixed up together and intensified. And you know each of those states encompasses your whole being."

"When does it happen?"

"Well, it happened the first time a couple years ago when I was away at the writer's conference I go to every spring. I don't think I ever told you this, but I met a woman there that year who had a daughter who used to have cystic fibrosis. It was all quite a coincidence because her daughter was the same age as you and even had the same name."

Peggie sat very still.

"There was no mistaking the diagnosis. In fact, when that Margaret was little she was much sicker than you've ever been. But Ruth — that was the woman's name — and her husband prayed for her, and all through the years they watched her improve. Till one day the doctor called Ruth into his office and said, 'I don't know how to tell you this, and I certainly can't explain it, but we've retested Margaret and she no longer has cystic fibrosis.' "

"Wow! You should have told me about that, mother."

"The doctor said that C.F. covered a broad spectrum and they could only see what went on in the center of the spectrum, and that with Margaret something had obviously gone on out on the edges where they couldn't see. Of course Ruth believed God healed Margaret."

"Wow! But you don't really think it was a coincidence that you met her, do you, mother?"

"No, I think it was one of *God's incidents* — one of the most outstanding of my life."

"Well, I should think so."

"At first I was so jealous. I hated Ruth because God had done that for her daughter and not for you," I said, not mentioning that the reason I hadn't told her about the other Margaret long ago was that I didn't want her to experience such jealousy. "That's when I was feeling guilty all the time, too, so naturally I figured it was because she had more faith than I did. But we became good friends, and at the end of the week we went to mass together."

"Was Ruth Catholic?"

"Yes, she was, and we knelt side by side in this beautiful little chapel and said together the prayer Catholics say at every mass:

> Holy, Holy, Holy, Lord
> God of Power and might,
> Heaven and earth are full of your glory.

"And I just knelt there next to Ruth and told God that if He chose to heal her Margaret and not mine that was His affair. That I would respect His reasons. That I was going to stop telling Him what to do, stop trying to use Him for my ends. That He was God, and He should command me. That I and my children would be at His disposal, and the only thing I asked was that in whatever corner of earth — or heaven — we occupied we might add in some measure to the fullness of His glory there.

"And that," I finished softly, "was when God first put His arms around me."

"Sometimes the way you say things, mother, you make me want to cry."

"There was one other special time when God held me very close," I went on, it not being often I had so enraptured an audience. "I was particularly worried about you and Joey right then — you know how I am — and wondering how I'd ever get along without you if I had to.

"You know," I added playfully, "with no one around to scribble up my shopping lists with smile faces — "

Peggie giggled. "And nobody spending all your money on clothes and then not wearin' them."

"Exactly. All kinds of things like that. Well, anyway, I was in church again, and I asked God if He could fill the kind of emptiness I'd feel if I did lose you — and He demonstrated what He would do."

"Now you're making me jealous."

"Well, I'm not saying God would take your place. I couldn't very well send God off to school in the mornings, could I? Or have mother-daughter talks with Him? Or watch His face light up on Christmas Day? But I think God was trying to tell me that if He relieves that awful cosmic loneliness that exists at the core of our beings, then we can, if we must, endure any other loneliness."

"You mean if God keeps us company, we can do without anybody else's company if we have to?"

"Yes, honey," I said, and found myself choking up before I knew what was happening. I guess because most of all I knew I was going to miss watching Peggie's incisive mind at work — that quick, intuitive perception that enabled her to take anything I said and re-say it in simpler, truer form.

"Now, mother, there's nothing to cry about."

"Well, I think we make a mistake if we don't realize there's going to be pain. If a Christian cuts his finger, it bleeds just like the non-Christian's. And if the Christian's heart is all cut to shreds, the pain's excruciating. Sometimes we tend to think the Holy Spirit is like some kind of anesthetic gas and if we just inhale enough of Him we won't feel any pain. Then when we do, we feel betrayed."

"Nuts!" said Peg. And then, "That part about the anesthetic, did you think that up all by yourself?"

"It comes out of experience, Peggie. Out of long experience."

"He'll help you take it, but He won't make it less. Except maybe 'cause He's helping you it might seem less. I'm surprised at you, mother, just learning that. I been knowin' it for a long time."

And then, I think because she feared the separation we'd been discussing more than she was ready to admit, she put her arms around my neck and gave me an impulsive hug. "I love you more than you love me," she said, beginning the baby game we'd played so often in days gone by.

"Oh, no, you don't," I replied. "I love you more than you love me."

"You do not! I love you more — "

"You're just trying to make me say it again."

"How did you know?"

"We all like to hear it."

"Do you think God likes to hear it?"

"I'm sure He does."

"It's kind of hard, though, mother. I mean you can't get close to Him like you can to a friend."

"Oh, I don't know," I told her, squirming a little on the hard step, "maybe closer. God can get right inside you. But you have to develop the knack of knowing He's there and listening to Him talk to you, as well as talking to Him."

"Like what you've been talkin' about when He hugs you?" Peg asked. "Now that's one thing I'm very guilty about. I don't have a time to talk to God. I mean not everyday regular. But I sure do like to talk to people."

"You're a lot better than I am about talking to people, Peg," I said, "about loving people and letting them love you." That was one thing I was learning, though, through all the emotional and financial strain of the children's illness — to find the strength I needed not only in an inner piety, but through the support of God's people as well.

"Well, that makes me feel good to be better than you at

something," Peg said. "I mean anybody wants to love me, I let 'em."

"You're a lot better than I am at a lot of things," I assured her. "But God seems to be working so hard to teach me to derive the help I need from horizontal as well as vertical relationships that I think this one way in which you're better must be very important."

Peg pondered that for a minute. "Gottcha, mom."

And then I told Peg one more story. Just a small happening that had taken place not long before when we'd gone back to our last church and stopped in to visit our old neighbor. The one with four kids and cancer, as Peggie referred to her. Just before we left, Joe asked her if Christ had become more real to her through her illness. She'd looked at him like he was out of his mind even to ask. "I used to know all about Christ," she said, "but now He's with me all the time."

Then she went on to tell us that she didn't even worry about her children any more because last Christmas when she'd been lying in bed doing what she could to wrap some presents and worrying about all the Christmases to come when she wouldn't be there to wrap and hide and whisper, she'd heard a voice.

"Oooooh! A voice?" squeaked Peg at this point in the narrative.

"Yes," I replied, "it was God's voice, and He said, 'If I'm taking care of you, don't you think I'll take care of your children?' And ever since then, whenever I'm tempted to be anxious about myself," to wonder, I added silently, how I'll survive the loss of both Peg and Joey, "I just reverse the words and hear God say, 'If I'm taking care of your children, don't you think I'll take care of you?'"

"I really can't comment, mother. I mean it's your problem you're talking about. Not mine."

"Well, I thought you might worry about me sometimes and that it would help you to know I'll be all right."

"Well, God's nice, mother. Of course I know He'll take

care of you. And the grandparents will help and the aunts and the people at the church."

"Okay. I'm sorry I brought it up. As long as you know."

"I know, mother. I know. I know."

Conversation About Reward In Heaven

"I Am What I Am 'Cause You Are What You Are"

Conversation About Reward In Heaven

"Guess what?" I said, reaching inside the mist tent where Peggie lay almost asleep and shaking her almost awake.

"What? What?" she demanded, knowing even in her groggy state that something portentous must have happened for *me* to be encouraging *her* to talk after bedtime.

"Mrs. Ruini just called, and she wants you to be a Bible School teacher this summer. Not a helper any more, but a regular, full-fledged, grown-up kindergarten teacher."

"Oh, mother, a teacher?" Peg breathed ecstatically, shocked into wakefulness. "Does daddy know? Me a teacher? But why me?"

"Well, Mrs. Ruini says she's been watching you with the children on Sunday mornings and you have very good craft ideas and very good lesson ideas and you're very enthusiastic and very respectful and — "

"Praise, praise, beautiful praise," Peggie chanted, emerging from her tent headfirst, hands clasped to her bosom. "Praise at last!"

"Come here, you silly thing," I laughed, sitting on the end of the bed and pulling her down beside me, wet head, clammy pajamas, and all. "My goodness, I don't know anyone who gets as much praise as you do. Why does working in that Sunday school mean so much to you anyway?"

Of course I knew why. For her psychologist had told us that Peggie's strong characteristics — her keen mind and highly developed conscience — were not assets in the junior high establishment. In high school she might find a small group of kids to whom she could relate, but for now she'd find her most meaningful relationships with older people and younger children. I guess I just wanted to know if Peggie knew why.

"Well, I get respect there," she said. "You know I seem big to them, and those little kids look up to me. I mean I walk in that kindergarten and they all come yelling *Peggie, this* and *Peggie, that*. It really makes you feel important."

I pulled up her fluffy quilt and tucked it in around us both as we settled back against the wall — Peggie lost, I was sure, in dreams of her encroaching super-importance as a teacher and I in my reflections on the importance Peggie placed on being important.

I'd been leafing through a *Reader's Digest* just that day, and there on the "How to Increase Your Vocabulary" page I'd come on Peg's rounded scrawl: "Peggie Woodson got 17 right — Sept. 2." It wasn't enough for her to do well. She had to record the fact for posterity.

I thought, too, of how she'd gotten a leave from the hospital the year before, a leave that entailed the removal and reinsertion of the dreaded i.v. in her arm, just so she could play "Beautiful Dreamer" all by herself at her band's Christmas concert. Only one other child had played a solo.

"Why did you volunteer?" I had asked.

"Well, how else would I be noticed?" Even group recognition wasn't enough for Peg.

Of course I understood that Peg's need for acceptance would be greater than the normal child's, as she felt different both physically and spiritually. Still I didn't know what to make of her attitude. For we Christians were to be a self-effacing folk, refusing first place, working for our fellow-man with no thought for reward, were we not? Didn't even our non-Christian society equate goodness with an absence of self-seeking? On the other hand, didn't the need for approval groan deep within us all, cover up its agony as we adults might? And wasn't Peggie's out-in-the-open begging for applause a healthier thing than our duplicity?

Then my mind moved to an incident that had occurred a week or two earlier. We'd been on our way, once again, to look for shoes for Peggie.

"Is that your new dress you're wearing, mother?"

"Yes, it is."

"It's like an old friend already, isn't it?"

"Yes, I'd say it is."

"You know the other night when we were shopping and you were wearin' that dress and you were walkin' around, I was lookin' at you and I was thinkin', *I'm not ashamed she's my mother.*"

"Well, thanks — I think."

"Course when you got up close I did notice the dress was wrinkled."

"I'll try to watch the wrinkles."

"I do think you have to be careful though about your attitude toward clothes, mother," Peg admonished me seriously. "I mean all these shopping sprees we're going on. You have to remember clothes aren't all that important. It's what's on the inside that counts."

"I'll try to remember about what's on the inside," I'd said.

And all at once I knew what I was doing there in the quiet of Peg's bedroom. I was rehearing a conversation that had been particularly rewarding to me as Peggie was probably rehearing the phone conversation with Mrs. Ruini that I'd just passed on to her.

And the reward I was experiencing wasn't just the intrinsic

type of reward we'd learned was acceptable in education courses in college. "Encourage your pupils to learn their arithmetic so they can count change at the store, not for a star on a chart," they'd said. Though it was intrinsic. For what mother could watch a daughter grow in beauty of character — inside, where it counts — and not know a satisfaction inherent in the effort of her motherhood?

It was extrinsic too. For what mother who for so long had trudged through a backwash of adolescent put-downs wouldn't thrill to such unmitigated tribute as "I'm not ashamed she's my mother," even if it was of the star-on-the-chart variety.

But then the Bible did talk about stars in our crowns, did it not? In fact, it talked an awful lot about rewards in general. Hadn't Jesus said we were blessed when we were persecuted for His sake because our reward was great in heaven? Hadn't He specifically urged us to store up treasure for ourselves in heaven, where moth and rust could not corrupt and thieves could not break in and steal? And hadn't Paul said he was striving to reach the end of the race so he could receive the prize for which God was calling him up to heaven?

Maybe it wasn't wrong to work for personal compensation — not if you worked for the right kind of payment, and went about earning it in the right way, and stashed it away in the proper place. True, Jesus had insisted that anyone who followed Him would have to deny himself, that anyone who tried to save his life would lose it. But hadn't He gone on to say that anyone who lost his life for His sake would find it? Wasn't the very reason He insisted on our focusing on others that He knew it was the only way we'd discover ourselves?

I came to a pause in my reflections then, and looking down at Peggie's face in the soft glow of her night light I knew I'd been right about what she'd been thinking. For there she was smiling to herself, grinning from forehead to chin, the scattered teardrops on her cheeks only adding to the rainbow of her joy.

"It means a lot to you, doesn't it, honey, what Mrs. Ruini said?" I asked tenderly.

"Well, wouldn't it mean a lot to you? I mean I been goin' down there every Sunday and workin' with those kids and I didn't even know anybody knew I was there. Just think, mother, I'm gonna be a teacher. Little ole me — a teacher."

"You know, Peg," I said, "often we think about dying and facing Judgment Day as a thing to be feared, a time of punishment for our sins. Maybe we should look on it more as a time of recognition. Can you imagine how you're going to feel when God Himself says to you, 'Well done, good and faithful servant. You've been faithful over ten children. I'll make you teacher of a hundred.' "

"Oh, mother, a hundred?" she wailed. "I don't think I could handle a hundred. That would be too much responsibility. I don't even know if I'd want Him to praise me if it'd mean drudging all day long. To me the nice part about being praised is just being noticed."

"Well, if that's where you are right now," I told her, "I think that's how you should conceive of judgment — as a kind of graduation day, a time when Jesus says, 'Well done, Peggie Woodson. Congratulations, Peggie Woodson.' "

"Yeah, I'd like that. And you know what else I think I'm gonna like about heaven? I think it's gonna be a place where everybody can do the thing he does best but without competition. Like everybody can be happy for everybody who gets highest honors. I mean I hate competition."

"Now that's a clever way to look at it, Peg," I said and felt her swell beside me. Could it possibly be, I wondered, that I didn't praise this child enough? That I was so anxious for her to grow so tall in the time she had that I communicated more anxiety over what she wasn't than respect for what she was? I was going to have to see that I affirmed Peg more. For if I wanted her to grow — well, that was a true thing they'd taught us in education courses: a child responds more to commendation than to criticism.

"Sometimes *I* tend to think we're supposed to love our neighbor more than we love ourselves," I told her. "But you're the one who's right. It's good for us to be happy about our own rewards as long as we're equally happy about our neighbor's."

"This thing about God praising you, mother. It's a little like what we were talking about at the Pancake House the other night, isn't it?" Peg asked. And then she snuggled up closer to me, and we both sank into our private reveries again.

Joe had been out of town for a few days, and I'd taken each child out to eat separately. It had been planned as a treat, but Peg's eyes had been tight as she looked at me over her menu, her forehead creased.

"You know Jim?" she asked, referring to a friend's son who had run away from home. "Suppose he dies while he's out there doin' wrong things. I mean I know he believes all the stuff you're supposed to believe, but is it enough to believe it or do you have to live a certain way?"

"Well, daddy always says we're not saved by faith alone or by works alone but by faith that works. That if we truly believe in Jesus, we will live in a certain way."

The waitress set Peggie's eighteen silver dollar pancakes, her hot chocolate, and her root beer float before her, but Peg continued to regard me apprehensively.

"Are you worried about Jim or yourself, honey?" I asked, and watched as she quickly lifted her napkin so no one could see her face crumble.

Oh, help me, Father, please, I prayed. Help me say the right thing to this child. Help me alleviate her fears.

"When I was your age, Peg," I told her, "I used to worry a lot about whether I was going to heaven or not, about whether I believed in Jesus just right. The bathroom was the only room in our house with a lock, and I used to shut myself in there all the time and ask Jesus to come into my heart over and over in case I hadn't asked Him right the last time. It was awful." I paused, and Peg nodded appreciatively.

"I was concentrating on what I felt *I* had to do," I went on. "Now when I'm tempted to worry about dying, I think about what God has already done. About how Jesus died to pay the penalty for our sins so death could be as harmless for the rest of us as a bee that's had its stinger removed. And I just say, *Lord have mercy*, and leave it up to Him whether or not He does. And when I leave it up to Him, what do you think — He does or He doesn't?"

Peg was crying openly now.

"Oh, honey, please don't cry," I urged. "You know there's something I've been thinking about over and over lately, a funny thing to be thinking about when it's cold out like it has been. Maybe God put it into my mind because it's something He wants me to say to you right now." I reached under the table and patted her knee, and she gave me a tremulous smile.

"What is it?" she asked.

"Well, you know every summer when I walk up the beach on Fire Island by myself? It's always seemed to me that the ocean was trying to tell me something about God, but I could never hear its message. Everybody always said the ocean spoke to them of the greatness and majesty of God, but I'd look and listen and think — No, that's not what it's saying to me.

"And then just the other day during that early snow I got to remembering how we sing the same hymn summer after summer when we visit different churches on vacation. One summer I swear we sang that hymn three Sundays in a row in three different churches, like God was hounding me with it. And all at once I knew — "

Oh, how could I best say it, I wondered, pausing as the waitress put a steaming cup of coffee down before me. "And all at once I knew the next time I knelt at the brim of the Atlantic and breathed its endlessness it would speak to me through the words of that hymn:

> There's a wideness in God's mercy,
> Like the wideness of the sea."

"Why didn't anybody ever tell me that before?" Peg challenged.

"A funny thing about that word *wideness*, though, Peg. As many times as I read it, I always read it wrong. I always sang,

'There's a *wildness* in God's mercy.' And I like it that way, too. Because now when I see the ocean in my mind, all the width and length of it surging and crashing at me, when I hear the deep howling to the deep, I say to myself, *I'll take my chances on the mercy of God."*

"You have to write that down, mother," Peg had said. "I mean put that in an article or something. Tell people about that."

I was glad now as we sat together on the end of her bed that Peg had remembered our Pancake House discussion. "Did it help you, honey, not to worry so much about dying — those things we talked about that night?" I asked.

"Well," she said, "I figure if God doesn't want me to go to hell and He's gonna do everything in His power to get me to heaven, and if I want to go to heaven and believe all the stuff, I got a three-to-one chance of getting there. I mean He's a lot more powerful than the devil and He's gonna do all He can to get me there, and I'm sittin' right here every day lettin' Him do it. I mean I try to let Him do what He wants every day, even though I don't always know what it is."

"How about that one chance in three?"

"Well, I figure that one chance is if I don't really believe the stuff in my heart and just want to go to heaven so badly I tell myself I believe it."

"There's more to that hymn I told you about the other night," I said. "I think you'd like it all. Some of it's even about judgment.

> There is no place where earth's sorrows
> Are more felt than up in heaven;
> There is no place where earth's failings
> Have such kindly judgment given.
> For the love of God is broader
> Than the measures of man's mind;
> And the heart of the Eternal
> Is most wonderfully kind."

Peggie pulled away from me then so she could see my face.

"You know, mother," she said, "sometimes I look at my morals and I wonder how you ever got them into me. And I try to analyze what you did so I can do the same thing to my kids — if I have any. So if God's gonna say to me what you've been telling me, *You did good, Peggie,* He'll have to say the same to you. 'Cause I've decided I am what I am 'cause you are what you are."

Then it was my turn to wipe the tears from my cheeks.

Conversation About Extended Life in Heaven

"And You Guys Didn't Want Me To Go!"

*Conversation About Extended
Life in Heaven*

How silent the house was, I thought, shutting the front door cautiously behind me and almost tiptoeing through the hollow rooms. How awesomely silent the house was.

And how silly you are, I told myself. True the eighth grade was going to Washington, and I'd just dropped Peggie off at the bus. But not true that the house was any emptier than any other day when I came back from dropping her off at school.

Yet as I walked about picking up the book Peg had left on the stairs and the book Peg had left on the teacart and the book Peg had left on the kitchen table, my footsteps echoed in what seemed unfurnished chambers. Did she ever have less than three books in the works at once, I wondered? Careful now not to let one little piece of napkin fall out. Heaven help me if I lost her places. Heaven help me if I lost any one of her places.

And then I stood in Peggie's room looking about helplessly for a vacant spot on which to pile the books. Looking about at a collage of clothes, papers, cheese crackers, and suitcases that for one reason or another had not been exactly right for

the long-anticipated, endlessly discussed, three-day-and-two-night, fifty-dollar field trip to Washington, D.C.

Oh, well, I thought, just this once — went and got a broom and swept everything sweepable into a compact mass in the middle of the floor, sat myself in front of it with wastebasket on one side and laundry basket on the other, and prepared to sort out all that was left to me for the moment of Peggie Woodson.

And then I buried my head in a rumpled housecoat and cried my heart out. Why hadn't anybody told me how much more you missed people when you worried about them? Aside from C.F. camp, where we knew Peg received more than adequate care, this was the longest we'd let her be away from us. "She can go," the doctor had said, "if she's careful not to get too tired." But how could she not get tired with the hectic schedule all day and the partying in the rooms at night? And how would she ever get enough to eat? The food was terrible on those trips. Hadn't the entire ninth grade been spreading its Washington-trip starvation stories for weeks? And they were kids with normal appetites.

What if Peg couldn't keep up with her friends and they left her behind? And her enemies. Suppose away from normal restraints they were more than normally cruel and she didn't have me to help her see herself in perspective?

Aimlessly I dropped a bunched-up white sock in the laundry basket, a month-old algebra assignment in the waste-basket. And then, speaking of collages, right on the floor in front of me was the collage of herself Peggie'd made for English class — a large cardboard covered with pictures and small objects designed to reveal the core of her personality and on the basis of which another student would write a theme on Peg's uniqueness.

There in the middle dominating the whole she'd pasted the jacket of her beloved *To Kill A Mockingbird*. And around it one flyer giving the public library hours and another listing the Caldecott medal winners for children's literature.

On top of the book cover she'd superimposed a near-perfect

progress report and half a page of the "Exodus Marching Overture" for B-flat clarinet. Glued about here and there were samples of her wheat penny collection, her license plate collection, the shell collection she added to at Fire Island every summer, the stamp collection she and her father worked on together, and the Snoopy card collection with which we all played so many wild games of four-handed solitaire. And glued about everywhere were pictures of food — stew and turkey and cake — even an open refrigerator bulging with all kinds of goodies. Then she'd found the words *cheese* and *potatoes* and taped them on for good measure. She'd given no hint of her health problem. Only someone close to Peg would know the lifesavers represented her effort not to cough at school.

Up in the left corner next to the pink barrette — "So they'll know I'm a girl, mother, with flyaway hair" — she'd pasted a picture of a TV set and beneath that a picture of our church, the two approximately equal in size.

Well, good for her for including the church at all, I thought.

Then she'd typed out a couple quotations and pasted them beneath the church. "I believe in the sun when it does not shine," said the first. "I believe in God when He is silent."

So she had her dark moments, too, did she?

And the second quotation, "If a man does not keep pace with his companions, perhaps he hears a different drummer."

Two bright red spots stood out. One a stick picture of a young girl teaching a group of little children and the other a birthday card with a red mouse on it. She'd gotten the card especially for her sixth grade teacher who was known far and wide for her love for *meeces* and whom Peg would always love with unqualified devotion. Peggie had told me the mouse card was going on her collage.

"But no one will know that stands for Miss Murdock," I said.

"I'll know," she replied.

And suddenly the house was empty again, missing as it did

that fierce fidelity of hers. And empty, I realized now, not just because Peg was on her way to Washington, but because this journey anticipated for me a longer journey she'd soon be taking, a journey from which she'd not return. When that time came — someone else would have to fish the dirty socks out from under the bed. For I would not. Could not.

I'd been on the escalator in Penney's a couple days before when from the floor above had come the cry of a small child for his mama. Such a cry of fright, such a frightful cry, that when I'd gotten off the escalator and seen the little fellow darting this way and that, shrinking from anyone who tried to help, I'd become physically ill. I never had been able to bear the cry of a lost child.

Would Peggie feel lost, I wondered, even for a moment when she *got off the bus* in heaven? It could be a terrifying experience — even a trip to see God — could it not, for a child alone? Especially an overly dependent, overly vulnerable, sensitive, sensitive, sensitive child?

And then from the diminishing mound in front of me I rescued Peggie's empty piggie bank and started a new pile for "miscellaneous items to be put back where they belong."

A young man in our church had died recently, unexpectedly, from a heart attack. He'd made a point of stopping to talk to Peg on Sunday mornings, once or twice stooping to kiss her cheek, and when she heard the church was making up a memorial gift for his family she came downstairs with four crumpled dollar bills, a quarter, two dimes, and three pennies clenched in her fist.

"I want you to put this in the plate for Bob," she said.

She'd done the same sort of thing back in the fifth grade when Mike, the school guard, had died. The other kids had given their nickels and dimes to buy a plaque in his honor, but Peg gave three months' allowance.

"What did the teacher say when she saw all that money?" I'd asked, suspecting she'd done it partly for show.

"Nobody knew, mother," she'd replied indignantly. It

seemed she'd been busy the week before Mike died and rushed past him without saying "Hi." "Just the day before he died, mother, I thought to myself, *I'll say hi to Mike tomorrow*, and then he wasn't there tomorrow.

"I want to give all I have," she'd said.

It gave her special pains, that sensitivity of hers. But a special productivity, too. And perhaps her own brand of purity as well.

Oh, I knew all mothers thought their children extraordinary, but Peg was extra extraordinary, and I wouldn't let the modesty I worked at as a parent deny it. After all, how many thirteen-year-olds had a library of 349 books, all properly indexed by author, title, and subject in strictest accord with the Dewey decimal system? And how many thirteen-year-olds read thirty, forty, fifty, even sixty books a month?

Exactly how many thirteen-year-olds were there who came to their mothers and said, "I've made a decision not to watch that program on TV any more. I mean I know there's nothing really wrong with it, but all the jokes are about sex and they make me feel that sex is dirty, and I don't want to feel that way. You know, mother, a lot of the kids at school go around huggin' each other in the halls. Now I don't think you should do that 'til you find the person you're gonna marry. Personally, I'm saving myself for the right man in college."

She marched to a different drummer all right. I'd given her that quotation on a bookmark last Christmas. She'd grasped its meaning immediately. "The kids at school keep askin' me about it," she told me later, "and I keep trying to explain, but they just don't get it."

Not that she was without flaws, I laughed to myself, unwadding a ball of paper before I tossed it in the wastebasket and seeing there in Peg's best printing, amidst many squiggles and yellow daisies the following tirade:

Joey is dumb.
Joey is stupid.
Joey is an idiot.

Joey is an ignoramus.
Joey is disgusting.
Joey is a prevaricator.
Joey is a procrastinator.

And not that the sorrow I felt at her absence wasn't mixed with relief. For she did still have a way of clinging to me. Were many chronically ill children like that, I wondered? Listening for the first squeak of your bedsprings in the morning, stepping on your heels all day long?

Yet how unbearably I'd miss her when she was no longer there to cling. How unbearably I'd miss watching her become that particular grand and great woman only she could become.

I extracted several paperbacks from the rubble heap. "No book should begin at the end," I declared, "or any child's life." There was so much knowledge I longed to see my daughter's mind acquire. Would there be time? Suppose she did *save herself for college* and time ran out?

Then my eyes went back to the collage, to the rusty diary key fastened to the lower right-hand corner. "Well, you know, mother," I remembered Peg saying, "what if I do become a famous writer when I grow up? People may want to know about my early days."

Surely anybody who could think up that many unpleasant adjectives for one small brother had potential as a writer. But would there be time for her to make her contribution in her field, to love her fellow-man maturely, wisely? There was so much loveliness in the world she needed time to look upon. So much happiness she hadn't yet the talent to lay hold of.

And what about me, I asked, adding a large *Introduction to the Physical Sciences* text to the book pile. I'd invested so much of myself in Peggie. Had I invested it all in an introduction — to nothing?

I thought about these things on and off during the next three days and two nights. Especially when Joey wasn't around and the quiet became too great and I had to think about them — think my way through them.

I read, for example, through all the sections in the Book of Revelation that describe heaven and discovered that as I listed all the things that would not be in heaven I was listing the things children most dislike. For there would be no crying in heaven. No hurting, no dying, no sadness of any kind. No night, no lostness. No unfairness, no lying, no stealing. No badness of any kind.

And then I began to think about what *would* be there, searching all through the Bible. The list was shorter, surprisingly, composed of two items mostly. The first and all-encompassing was *love*. How could I, who claimed in any measure to know Jesus, have thought that even for the briefest second He'd let Peggie wander in gray, chilling fogs? I remembered how when she was little she'd climb up in my lap and ask what it was like to die, the very innocence of her question only adding to the weight of my knowledge. My answer had always been the same. "Well, the first thing that happens is Jesus takes you on His knee and rocks you."

No, I wouldn't be with her. Good! For He would. No longer would she be subject to my puny, partial love. She would be loved wholly, and not just by God, but by all the human creatures who, like Peg, would now be free themselves to love — enough.

The second item on my list was *continuity*, by which I meant the continuation of each individual personality. Though it was hard for me to see this at first, brainwashed as I'd been to think we'd all be carbon copies of each other in heaven, sitting around on identical clouds strumming assembly line harps.

But I remembered something the preachers had always said when I was growing up — about eternal life being a present thing, a quality as much as a quantity of life. "Whoever believes in the Son," they quoted John, *"has* everlasting life and shall not pass into darkness but *has passed* from death unto life." "The life you experience with God after death," they said, "is only an extension of the life you experience with Him now."

I think I believed this emotionally at first because I needed so badly to believe it, and perhaps that was reason enough. But Joe was a great help to me in this period, and in the end I believed it because of a biography he pointed out to me, a biography that enabled me actually to compare the life of someone before and after physical death.

That someone, of course, was Jesus. Joe asked me to study His outstanding personality traits as He dealt with His disciples before His death and then to do the same thing as He dealt with them after His death. I could discern no difference in His personality at all. His relationships, even His vocabulary, went unchanged.

Then Joe reminded me of the episode where Peter and the other disciples had been fishing all night and caught nothing, and Jesus told them to cast their nets on the other side of the boat. Episodes I should say, because there were two of them, one occurring near the beginning of Jesus' ministry and one after the Resurrection. Episodes not identical but so similar that some scholars thought Jesus' biographers had made a mistake and recorded the same incident in different places.

Most inspiring to me, though, was Jesus' appearance to two of His disciples on the Emmaus Road. If Christ had been anything in His pre-death lifetime, He'd been a teacher. And here He was again, unable to restrain Himself, opening the Scriptures to His disciples, doing His teaching thing. And they knew Him. They thought Him dead, and He never told them who He was — but in the end they knew Him. "Oh, didn't our hearts burn within us," they asked, "as He walked with us and talked with us in the way?"

I had not been wrong to long for fulfillment for my children, except perhaps in the sobriety of my longing. I had only been wrong in my judgment of where they could find it.

And so I came to know with my most basic "knower" that the particular charm that was Joseph Woodson, Jr., that the ferocious loyalty and generosity, the depth of the feeling and heights of the neatly catalogued thinking that pulsed within the fragile frame of Margaret Ann Woodson would not change at death, but only grow, only expand in an atmosphere more energetic than any I could provide. And the hearts of all who walked and talked with her on her transfigured way would burn within them as she did her Peggie Woodson thing.

And all of this forevermore. Where no child's pleasure would ever be dimmed by the words, "We have to go now." And no adult ecstasy would ever be made grievous by a raven's mournful "nevermore." And no mother would ask, "Will there be time?" Only an ending like death could be called endless beginning. Of all the silly things in the world of which to be afraid, death was the silliest.

And then the days of my travail were ended, and I was back at school waiting for Peg to return from Washington.

"I'm waiting for my daughter, Peggie Woodson," I said to the woman next to me. "She's on the number three bus. I'm a little anxious because she has cystic fibrosis, and the school nurse said the kids get awfully hot on the bus and when they get off at the Tomb of the Unknown Soldier it's windy and — " And then my voice trailed off, and I sauntered away to the shelter of the damp brick walls. "Nothing like making a complete idiot of yourself," I mumbled, thankful for the dark shadows that hid my tears. "Haven't you learned anything while Peg's been gone?"

And then the number three bus roared in.

And as the days wore on, I wished for a little quiet in the house.

"That bus I was on, mother? Well, it was a funny thing, but that was the Catholic bus. You know we let the kids from St. Joseph go with us every year. And it was just them on the bus and me and my friends. And the Catholic kids didn't know I had C.F. and they said *Hi* to me 'n all.

"Wait till you see all the pictures I took, mother. I mean the Lincoln Memorial and the Washington Monument and the White House and the Capitol. A lot of the kids acted like it was dumb to be patriotic. But, oh, mother, I couldn't tell you how I felt standing right there in front of the Capitol of my country.

"They had a lot of books everywhere, mother, but I couldn't buy them because I spent most of my money on daddy's back scratcher, but I got all these free booklets. Come here and let me show you how I'm putting them in my file cabinet. Did I show you this one on the Smithsonian? Oh, I did? Well, how about this one on the Wax Museum?

"Somebody had told the chaperone on my bus about me, mother. Do you think daddy did that? Anyway, she was so nice. I mean she didn't make me stand out or anything, but, well, like the day we stopped at this fried chicken place for supper and I told her I couldn't eat fried chicken and she said she'd get me a hamburger somewhere and I said could she make it two cheeseburgers and she did, mother. She bought me two cheeseburgers — with her own money."

And then one night when it had all been told and retold, all the wonders of "the best time of my life," Peg bristled her way into the bedroom where Joe and I sat propped in bed, innocently reading, and planted herself before us, arms crossed accusingly.

"And just to think," she sputtered, "just to think, you guys didn't want me to go!"

Conversation About Happiness in Heaven

"Of Course I Know I'm Gonna Like Heaven."

Conversation About Happiness in Heaven

"Oh, mother, that was the best movie!" Peggie cried, bobbing up and down on my bed and jouncing me out of what from the start had been an ill-fated nap. "I mean even you would have liked it. I know because this really old man — no offense, mother, he was more like a grandfather — came and sat next to me, and he was so fat he lapped over my chair and I had to hold my arm right in front of me and he was so jolly and kept laughin' so hard my whole chair was shakin'."

Thus Peggie launched into a blow-by-blow description of every funny thing that happened off the screen and on that Saturday afternoon. And I lay there laughing in response to her laughter and basking lazily in the happy glow that emanated from her.

I used to think teen-age hilarity was nothing but a front, a cover-up of that painful teen-age insecurity. I'm sure it is in part, but more and more I've been impressed with the natural-ness of the giggling syndrome of Peggie's age group. Life hasn't worn them down yet. The playfulness of the kitten is still upon them.

"You're really going to enjoy heaven, you know that, Peg?" I asked as she came up for breath.

It seemed a natural enough question to me, but Peggie gave me a long, quizzical look. "Will you excuse me please?" she asked politely. "I mean that was a long movie, and I really do have to go to the bathroom." And she took off for the half-bath off our master bedroom before I had a chance to reply.

I rolled over and pulled the pillow down on top of my head. She didn't have to go to the bathroom as long as she was talking about the world of Disney, but bring up the next world and she just couldn't wait — to go to the bathroom, that was. It was a reversal of the way things should be. It bothered me that Peg of all people shouldn't be glad over the gladness that waited for her in heaven.

It bothered me not a little, and sleep eluded me again as the reactions of certain characters in a booklet I'd been reading sounded through my mind. Reactions of a man and a woman, real-life people, who had died, stayed dead medically for several minutes, and then returned to life and recorded what they'd seen of the life beyond.

"Light! Love! Beauty! Peace!" The words ricocheted noisily in my empty brain till finally I gave up, reached for the *Guideposts* booklet in the headboard of my bed, and read again the accounts that had so impressed me. "Light" was what the back-to-lifers first encountered. At least they called it light. "I say light," said the man, "but there is no word in our language to describe brilliance that intense."

"I emerged into an overwhelming wide space of light," said the woman, "a pulsing, living light which cannot be described in words." Light that penetrated their beings with love and joy.

The "room was flooded, pierced, illuminated, by the most total compassion I have ever felt," said the man. "It was a presence so comforting, so joyous and all-satisfying, that I wanted to lose myself forever in the wonder of it."

"What I saw," said the woman, "made all earthly joys pale into insignificance. I longed to join the merry throng of children singing and frolicking in an apple orchard. The air had a brilliant clarity that made small details stand out in a new light: the orchard in translucent white and pinks, startling shades of greens, reds, yellows and russets. As I sat there drinking in the beauty, gradually I became aware of a Presence: a Presence of joy, harmony, and compassion." Neither wanted to come back. "That other world was far more real to me than the one to which I had returned," said the woman.[1]

"The lure of that heavenly place that I had glimpsed was very strong. The cry of my heart that moment has been the cry of my heart ever since," said the man. "Christ, show me Yourself again."[2]

I couldn't help noticing, even in my drowsy state, that these and other similar accounts I'd read from time to time all agreed in one respect. None of *the tellers* could fully describe the irresistible pull they felt toward the light, the singing, the children's laughter, the sweetness of the love of another element of life more alive than any they had lived and more loving than they as earthlings could endure.

That's what I wanted for Peggie — to feel that pull. She'd always had a special affinity for light-hearted folk. Little yellow smile faces had become her trademark. Why, she wouldn't even let us put up the warm, heavy drapes we planned to hang in her room because she wanted to waken in the morning with the sunlight dancing on her face.

My frustration grew as I tossed about, and I found myself remembering with unusual distinctness certain phrases C.S. Lewis had put into the mouth of Ransom, his earth man, as Ransom wandered through the unspoiled joys of the distant

---

[1] "The Window of Heaven" by Julia Phillips Ruopp, *Guideposts,* October 1963. Reprinted by permission from *Guideposts* magazine, Carmel, New York.

[2] "Return From Tomorrow" by George C. Ritchie, Jr. M. D. Used by permission.

planet Perelandra. "The soft, almost impalpable caresses of the long thin leaves on his flesh, the low, singing, rustling, whispering music, and the frolic movement all about him." There was "a last touch of wildness" to the pleasure he experienced, an almost formidable quality. "There was something in Perelandra that might overload a human brain." And Perelandra wasn't even heaven. Just a planet like our own, *unbent* by sin.

That's what I had to communicate to Peggie — heavenly pleasures so intense that to take more than one sip at a time would be vulgar, orgiastic. And communicate it I would.

"Put your book down and come on out, honey," I called. "I have a couple questions for you."

"What questions?" Peg asked, emerging from the depths slowly, book held behind her back.

"Number one: If you had to make a choice between going to visit your jolly grandfather of this afternoon or God, which would you choose?" Now that had to be the least intelligent question of all time, and I can only put it down to my over-anxiety to make Peggie see how off-center her priorities were.

"Well, let's see," she answered, a note of secret amusement in her voice. "If I really had to make a decision, of course I'd say *God*. But if you want my immediate, off-the-cuff reaction, I'll say *Jesus*. Second question?"

"Now wait a minute," I protested, not willing to be outwitted so quickly by an answer obviously more sensible than my question. "Why do you say Jesus? What kind of person do you think He was?"

"At what time of His life? I mean in the Garden of Gethsemane or when?"

Smart-alecky she may be, I thought, but stupid she is not. And I took satisfaction in the fact that no static, mechanical-type Christian was developing here, no puppetlike creature who, once realizing a Christian was supposed to be joyous, would go about with a smile pasted on her face under every kind of circumstance.

"I think He *laughed* a lot, if you want to be *serious*," she said cutely, that pesky air of suppressed merriment still in her tone. "And He was always goin' around tellin' people how to be happy. Like that was His main thing. Next question?"

"Well, okay," I said, determined to make a better showing second time around. "If you had to explain to another person the difference between the good times of heaven and the good times of earth, how would you do it?"

That one took her a full sixty seconds. "Well, of course it would depend on the person. If it was someone like me, I'd say it was the difference between a McDonald hamburger and a sirloin steak. I mean you know me and food. And if it was someone like you, I'd say it was the difference between reading C.S. Lewis down here and talking to him in person up there."

I must have stared at her agape, for she burst out laughing, banging her fists on the bedspread in an absolute fit of hilarity. "I knew what you were doin'," she whooped, "from the minute you said, *Did I know I was gonna enjoy heaven?* I just thought I'd teach you a little lesson that I'm not so dumb as you think. Of course I know I'm gonna like heaven."

"Well," I said defensively, "maybe most people would choose heaven over hell, but I bet 99 percent of the population would choose earth over heaven if they had a choice. Come on now, don't most of the kids you know think perfection is just a little dull?"

"If I did have that idea, where do you think I got it?"

"Not from me!"

"Well, I must say people around here aren't exactly having the time of their lives being good."

"Ha to you," I said, but she'd struck home again. What I was spoke much more loudly to her than what I said.

"Actually, mother," she added in a more serious manner, "I know what you mean about the way most people feel. I used to think that way myself. But I changed. I mean I had to."

"What changed you?"

"Well, I guess you forgot, but once you were writing an

article on *Joy and Jesus* and you were tellin' me what a sunny person Jesus must have been for the children to like to be around Him. I never forgot that.

"And once when I was sad daddy read to me out of the Bible about *Be of good cheer* and *Blessed are they that mourn* and all and I told him that didn't make me feel a bit better and then he read me the same things out of a new Bible, and do you know what Jesus actually went around saying all the time? *Cheer up. Cheer up.* Like a bird, mother. And He didn't really say *blessed.* He said *fortunate* are those who do this or that. Daddy said if you wanted to translate it into junior high talk you could even say, *Boy, are you lucky, you guys who think pure thoughts,* and stuff like that. I mean who wants to go around being *blessed?*"

"That old-fashioned language does get in the way, doesn't it?" I asked. "I know it used to make me feel that what the Bible called joy was so different from what people today call happiness that I'd need a whole new inner apparatus to experience it. And that while I wanted what people today call happiness, I didn't really want what the Bible called blessedness or joy."

"Hey, just like me," Peg squealed. "What changed your mind?"

"Well, I think more than anything those times I told you about when God holds me tight. I learned firsthand that the love of God affects you like any other love, only more so, and that the pleasure you feel when you're with Him is like any other pleasure only somehow it's all you need."

How I wished I could explain it more fully. C.S. Lewis described heaven as a place where any little thing we wanted in our most deprived moments on earth would be there beyond our imaginings. Peggie would take one step inside the door and know she belonged, know she was where she'd always wanted to be. Where she'd find all the things she'd always longed for, elevated not into something other, but something *more.*

"The thing that means the most to me," Peggie said, "is something I heard some minister say once. That a rose will still be a rose in heaven, but it'll smell ten times sweeter. I mean I used to try to figure out what it would be like, but I decided it was just better than anything I could imagine so I forgot about it."

Maybe some day I'd stop feeling obligated to explain things to Peg, I thought. Maybe some day. "Do you ever get all excited when you think about going to heaven and just can't wait?" I asked.

But this time Peg looked at me uncomfortably. "Do you?" she countered.

"Just a short time ago I began to."

"Well, of course, you had to — what with your age and all."

I threw my pillow at her, but she was quicker than I in body as well as mind and the pillow thudded harmlessly into the door as she slammed it behind her.

I sank back in bed feeling older then I cared to feel. But, then, I consoled myself — you can't be over the hill, not if it's the hill to heaven you're climbing. For that's Happiness Hill. And Happiness Hill is nothing but uphill — all the way.

Conversation About What C.F. Really Means

"Are You Sure God's Like Daddy?"

Conversation About What C.F. Really Means

"You see," Peggie whispered triumphantly, "I always told you cemeteries were like this. I mean pretty, peaceful places." She danced about, hands upraised, an enchanted visitor in a magic fairyland.

It was Easter vacation and the start of a two-day stay in historic Philadelphia. I could appreciate Peg's delight. Getting there had been awful. The turnpike was crowded and noisy, and driving through the heart of Philadelphia had been a nightmare all its own. But here we were, half a block from our tenth-story room in as modern a brick and concrete Holiday Inn as existed in the twentieth century, transported into another time, another space.

A space shut in by ancient, black, iron fence and spreading, century-gnarled trees. An eighteenth century time, a springtime in which gold-green buds could no longer contain themselves and *quickened* starlings twittered ecstatic tunes. Watching Peg as she tiptoed through the tombstones, I

couldn't help remembering the words Adoniram Judson, the famous missionary, said at his death: "I go with the gladness of a boy bounding away from school."

"I always knew cemeteries were nice," Peg hissed persistently in my ear. Her indignation was mounting, but even she could not shout in this quiet, aged spot. "In our last church you used to take us walking in a cemetery, and I always remembered how peaceful it was. But would you believe me? No, you wouldn't believe me!"

I couldn't help chuckling as she skipped off. When Peg was amenable she was very, very amenable, but when she was obstreperous — she was impossible. Anyway, it wasn't a day for waving one's arms in protestations of innocence. It was a day for spreading wide one's arms and hugging close the warm, moist dirt smells of new life, of springtime both temporal and eternal.

I found a flat, raised marker and sat down on my own temporary resting place. We had it all to ourselves, we four Woodsons, this hushed, time-hallowed burial ground. Joe and Peg in earnest conversation in the corner where Joe had been examining the oldest of the monuments. Joey eyeing a particular grave with unusual preoccupation. Joe hugging Peg. Peg making her way slowly back to me over the crooked cobblestones, stooping to smell the wild roses nested in unplanned profusion against the cracked marble slabs.

She scootched up happily next to me. "I told daddy what I wanted on my tombstone," she said confidentially.

"Oh?"

"Yeah. I told him, *Absent from the body, present with the Lord.*"

I put my arm around her shoulders. Skinnier than ever they were, those skinny arms of hers. Yet how grateful I felt for all that had happened to her in the past year, all the prayers we'd prayed for her body being transferred it seemed to her ever-expanding spirit.

"You know how to make your father happy, don't you?" I asked.

"I think he liked it," she admitted smugly. "But I didn't say it just for that. I mean I like it, too."

Cool breezes played with our hair, and Peg, always so sensitive to the heat, sighed contentedly. "You're sure God's like daddy — right, mother?"

"Well, it might be better to say daddy's just a little bit like God."

"Mmmm — gotcha, mom."

"You remember back when you were having all that trouble at school with Eugene?" I asked. "You have no idea what a time I had with your father. He'd take one look at your face when you walked in, and he wouldn't even have to ask how things went. He'd get so mad. He was going to take Eugene's parents to court. He was going to find Eugene and beat him black and blue. I practically had to put him in restraints."

Peggie giggled delightedly. "I don't see why anybody should be afraid of dyin' if God's like daddy, do you, mother? Unless it's that Eugene," she added, eyeing me mischievously. And then she hopped down and ran to join Joey.

But soon she came tearing back to me. "Do you know what he's doing?" she cried breathlessly. "Do you know? He's takin' the pennies *off* Ben Franklin's grave. I mean you're supposed to put them on, and he's over there fillin' his pockets. You've got to do something about him, mother. I mean you have got — to — do — something — about — that — Joey!"

It was true. I had to do something about him, happy-go-lucky, conscienceless kid that he was. He'd never be another Peggie, though. I'd never be able to talk to him the way I did to her. But then he didn't give me the problems she did either, self-accepting, self-contained child that he was. And he did give so much of his own particular brand of pleasure. Never, ever could I choose between the two.

"Mother says to put every one of those pennies right back where you got them!" Peggie's roar carried across the length and breadth of the sacred *sleeping place,* indignation — and envy, too, I think — overcoming inhibition.

"Peggie!" I gasped. But my horror lasted only a minute before we both burst into subdued laughter.

"You know it is peaceful here," Peggie said, "but it's sad, too. I mean have you noticed how many of the markers are for little children? There's one right over there for Jennifer somebody, aged 2 years, 4 months, 6 days, and all like that. You know, mother, I been wonderin' — if I die at thirty, do you think maybe part of the purpose could be in the book you're writing?"

"It would be nice to think so."

"You know sometimes when I'm daydreaming I get this crazy idea. Like what if the book turned out to be a kind of advertisement for C.F., and people sent a lot of money and one day we could take it and dump it all in Dr. Rathburn's lap and tell him, 'Go find a cure for C.F.' Can you imagine the look on his face?"

We sat quietly for a minute imagining the look on Dr. Rathburn's face. And then Peg nudged me playfully. "About that book you're writing, mother — any more questions for my great mind?"

I nudged her right off the tombstone.

Just then the rumble of some particularly heavy traffic reached right inside our sanctuary. "You know I been wonderin', mother," Peg said again, "what you meant on our way here every time you kept saying, 'There goes another C. F. truck.' You acted like they were something special, but I looked on the trucks and C. F. just meant Consolidated Freightways."

"Well, they were something special to me, Peg," I replied. "It used to be that every time I drove past one of those C.F. trucks just for a minute I'd think they were full of children with cystic fibrosis. And I'd get kind of weak all over. I guess you might say C.F. used to mean *c*onstant *f*ear to me."

"And now?"

"Well, now after all the talks we've had this year, every time I see one of those trucks I think how *c*ared *f*or we are."

"Hey, neat!" Peg exclaimed. And then she pulled me over to the gate and pointed to a plaque fastened to the fence beside it. On it was the epitaph Benjamin Franklin had written for his own gravestone.

The body of
Benjamin Franklin, Printer,
Like the cover of an old book,
Its contents torn out,
And stript of its lettering and gilding,
Lies here, food for worms,
But the work shall not be lost,
For it will, as he believ'd,
Appear once more
In a new and more elegant edition,
Corrected and improved
By the Author.

"I read it when we first came in," Peg said, awe in her voice. "Do you think I was meant to see it? I mean me lovin' books the way I do?"

I couldn't answer for a minute.

"Now, for goodness sake, mother, don't go gettin' all choked up again. You're *cared for*, remember?"

She patted my shoulder in a mixture of impatience and comfort, so anticipatory of the time when in my dotage I'd be the child and she the adult that I broke down altogether. For, of course, that time would never come for us. We'd be alone in our old age, Joe and I. Our children had no earthly future we could plan with them. We'd never hold our grandchildren on our laps.

"*Cared for*, yes, honey," I said. "But not *care free*. Remember those drops of blood Jesus sweat? You couldn't exactly call that a *no sweat* attitude now, could you?"

"I know what you mean," she said. "You know I used to think I'd like to have a button that said *Live Every Day Like It's Your Last*. 'Cause I kept forgettin' it all the time and I didn't think I should forget. But lately I been thinkin' — No! Talk about it; then forget it. I mean I think we should think all about it and then go do something. Enjoy ourselves. Especially," she added significantly, "on vacation."

And then the two Joes came and joined us at the gate.

"Know what C.F. means?" asked Peg.

"Cat fish?" snickered Joey.

"No dummy. *C*ared *F*or. That's what C.F. means. *C*ared *F*or.

"I'll buy that," Joe said.

And the four of us walked out of the cemetery and into the world outside.